PRIMO LEVI

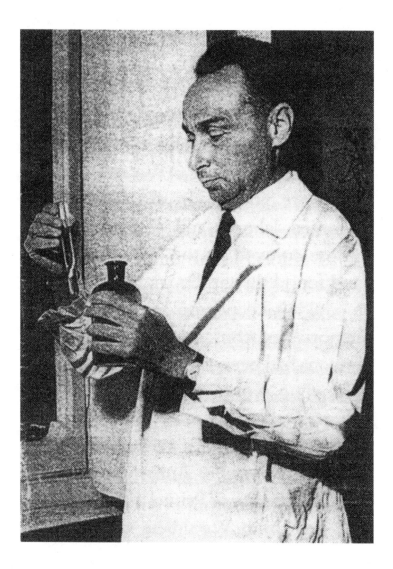

Primo Levi

The Matter of a Life

BEREL LANG

Yale

UNIVERSITY

PRESS

New Haven and London

Yale University Press books may be purchased in quantity for educational,
business, or promotional use. For information, please e-mail sales.press@yale.edu
(U.S. office) or sales@yaleup.co.uk (U.K. office).

Set in Janson type by Integrated Publishing Solutions,
Grand Rapids, Michigan. Printed in the United States of America.

Library of Congress Cataloging-in-Publication Data

Lang, Berel.
Primo Levi : the matter of a life / Berel Lang.
pages cm. — (Jewish Lives)
Includes bibliographical references and index.
ISBN 978-0-300-13723-1 (alk. paper)
1. Levi, Primo. 2. Jews—Italy—Biography. 3. Holocaust
survivors—Italy—Biography. I. Title.
PQ4872.E8Z724 2013
853'.914—dc23
[B]
2013018411

A catalogue record for this book is available from the British Library.

This paper meets the requirements of ANSI/NISO Z39.48–1992
(Permanence of Paper).

10 9 8 7 6 5 4 3 2 1

"I tried to explain . . . that the nobility of Man lay in making himself the conqueror of matter, and [that] I wanted to remain faithful to this nobility. That conquering matter is to understand it, and understanding matter is necessary to understanding the universe and ourselves."

———————

"Chemistry led to the heart of Matter, and Matter was our ally precisely because the Spirit, dear to Fascism, was our enemy."

—Primo Levi

Books by Berel Lang

Art and Inquiry
The Human Bestiary
Philosophy and the Art of Writing
Act and Idea in the Nazi Genocide
The Anatomy of Philosophical Style
Writing and the Moral Self
Mind's Bodies: Thought in the Act
Heidegger's Silence
The Future of the Holocaust
Holocaust Representation: Art Within the Limits of History and Ethics
Post-Holocaust: Interpretation, Misinterpretation, and the Claims of History
Philosophical Witnessing: The Holocaust as Presence

Edited/Co-edited Volumes

Marxism and Art
The Concept of Style
Philosophical Style
The Philosopher in the Community
The Death of Art
Writing and the Holocaust
Race and Racism in Theory and Practice
Method and Truth
The Holocaust: A Reader

For Barbara Estrin

Interlocutor: *But surely, M. Godard, you would agree that every film should have a beginning, a middle and an end.*

M. Godard: *Yes, of course—but not necessarily in that order.*

CONTENTS

PRIMO LEVI

I

The End

"It is particularly difficult to understand why a
person kills himself, since generally speaking the
suicide himself is not fully aware."
—Primo Levi, "Jean Améry, Philosopher and
Suicide," *La Stampa*, December 7, 1978

ON JULY 31, 1987, Primo Levi would have turned sixty-
eight, but he had died three and a half months earlier, on April
11, in the same apartment building on Turin's Corso Re Umberto where he was born and where, except for two intervals,
he had lived continuously since. One of those intervals was related to jobs he took after completing his university studies in
chemistry in 1941, work that took him to Milan. After that came
the two-year period that included his time with the partisans
and capture by the Italian Fascists, eleven months as a *Häftling*
(prisoner) in Auschwitz, and his lengthy post-liberation return

to Turin. The physician called by police to the scene of his death termed it a suicide, and that verdict was later affirmed by a Turin court. The cause of death was judged to be a fall from the landing of Levi's apartment on the third floor (the fourth, in American count) to the ground floor about fifty feet below. There was no evidence of criminal responsibility, and there were no eyewitnesses. The verdict of suicide was thus an inference, opening space for speculation that quickly filled with dissent—opposition to the verdict on one side and, on the other, disagreement among those who accepted the verdict but disputed the act's causes. Both responses led to pronouncements on Levi's life as much as on his death.

In Levi's closest circle of family and friends, reaction to his suicide mingled shock and grief with an awareness that approached resignation. A number of intimates had anticipated that end; the depression they saw engulfing him in the months previous was deep and sustained, even if not unbroken. Levi himself spoke and wrote about his depression, variously naming the factors that he saw contributing to it. Among these: Levi's mother, Rina (Ester), aged ninety-one and owner of the family apartment—a gift to her upon her wedding to which Levi and his wife, Lucia, had "temporarily" moved soon after their marriage—had been paralyzed for nine months by a stroke. In uncertain health for years before this, she increasingly demanded his presence in addition to that of hired aides (she would outlive her son by four years). Levi's mother-in-law, Beatrice Morpurgo, who lived in an apartment within walking distance, was ninety-five and had been virtually blind for fifteen years, requiring Lucia's continued attention. Levi had recently begun to consider moving his mother to a nursing home, but his sense of obligation resisted the change, with Lucia adding her objections to it. (Agnese Incisa, an editor at Einaudi and a friend of Levi's, had reproved him, "Either you die or your mother dies" —a locution he would himself later repeat.) The strain of these demands sharpened tensions in Levi's relationship with Lucia that were of long standing; with rare openness about this personal matter, Levi in midlife described it in some detail to one of his correspondent friends.[1]

To these external factors, Levi's body in 1987 added its own weight. Foot ulcers, perhaps vestigial from Auschwitz where he first experienced them, reappeared; shingles that surfaced first in 1978 now recurred. In mid-February, he underwent surgery for an enlarged prostate, and on March 18, the complication of a bladder blockage required further surgery (again under general anesthesia) and ten additional days in the hospital. There is some question of whether there were two operations or one, but none about the problem itself. No evidence of cancer was found in these procedures, but Levi remained apprehensive; in the aftermath he mentioned a problem with incontinence— a common effect of prostate surgery, but distressing nonetheless. Beyond such specific challenges, Levi had begun to fear that his memory and powers of concentration were failing, the remarkable faculties on which his work and expressive presence had drawn so readily. And then, too, there was a history of depression itself which extended to pre-Auschwitz days and only underscored the severity of this newest appearance. The regular pattern found in depressions of building on their own impetus added its increments here in his last days as well; the variety of anti-depressant drugs to which Levi turned seemed increasingly ineffective and all the more frustrating because of that.

Such factors would have had different weights, but their collective impact cannot be doubted: individual issues among them might have sufficed as causes or reasons for suicide—if there is indeed any way of generalizing about that. Levi's younger sister, Anna Maria, would insist after his death that the assembly of possibilities could be reduced entirely to one, namely, the prostate operation and its consequence. In any event, to recognize the cumulative effect of the factors noted does not diminish the challenge each posed individually.

But what then of the eleven months that Levi endured in Auschwitz forty-two years earlier? Did not also *that* enter and affect this final siege? Asked this question by several friends aware of the grip of his depression close to the end, Levi explicitly ruled that source out. Without denying the shadow of the "Lager" (the term he often used for Auschwitz or collectively for the camps), he ascribed *this* depression to what he took to be more proximate causes, and he offered the same assessment in other communications during his last weeks. Thus, he described the depression to Ruth Feldman, the American translator of his poetry: "In certain respects, it's even worse than Auschwitz"—at once comparing and contrasting the present with that past.[2] And surely, if explanations by means of sufficient cause *ever* explain suicide, the aggregate of factors cited would suffice even without the additional reference to Auschwitz. Viewed from the outside, depression often seems overdetermined, but even so, the weight of factors affecting Levi in this last period seems heavier than most. Admittedly, his own enumeration of the causes is not conclusive: reasons do not automatically count as causes, and even reasons named by the person affected can be disputed. Suicide notes—and Levi did not leave one—are inconclusive; even there, statements of intention or design do not have the last word in determining cause.[3]

Despite the weight of these considerations, claims attributing Levi's suicide to his months in Auschwitz surfaced quickly. Elie Wiesel's concise reaction epitomized this pattern: "Levi died at Auschwitz forty years later." (Wiesel's earlier recollection of having encountered Levi in Auschwitz was met by Levi's denial of any corresponding memory.)[4] And reactions similar to Wiesel's were expressed by other public figures, some of whom had known Levi personally (Natalia Ginzburg), others slightly

(Alberto Moravia) or not at all (Bruno Bettelheim), and widely in the Italian and foreign press. For them and still more for readers acquainted with Levi through his first two books—*If This Is a Man*, his account of the eleven months in Auschwitz, and *The Truce*, the narrative of his post-liberation return to Turin—the link between his suicide and Auschwitz appeared self-evident. Emanuele Artom, the rabbi of the Turin Jewish community of which Levi was a member, who conducted Levi's funeral, had rather different reasons for quickly judging Levi's death a "delayed homicide": quickly, in order to meet the Jewish requirement of burial within twenty-four hours of death or as near that as possible; "homicide" because Jewish law forbids burial of suicides in the common ground of the Jewish cemetery, requiring a separation in death from the community. Religiously, he had also to consider the requirement that in the event of doubt about the person's state of mind in the act, the verdict of suicide must be withheld.[5]

And then, too, those who dissented entirely from the verdict of suicide found a number of more specific reasons for that view, either in additional evidence or in reinterpreting the same evidence. Some among this group claimed (and still continue to hold) that for Levi to commit suicide would diminish or contradict too much else in his life and work, what he had lived through and for. An implication of this view is a contention that he *should not* have done it or, more strongly, that he *could not* have done it. But the first of these is a moral or psychological not a historical claim, and any version of *could not* is patently rhetorical. On the other hand, individual claims among the dissents warrant attention. So Rita Levi-Montalcini, a longtime friend of Levi's (herself a Nobel laureate in physiology or medicine in 1986), detected no hint of suicide in a conversation with Levi shortly before his death; more deliberately, she argued that someone as considerate as Levi was—*and* a professional chemist—would have found a less disturbing means of committing suicide if indeed he had decided to do that. The novelist Ferdinando Camon, though first accepting the suicide verdict, changed his mind on receiving a letter from Levi several days after the death in which Levi wrote with confidence about future plans: a counter-indicator, in Camon's opinion, to the official judgment.

But these, like all the other demurrals, offer no explanation of Levi's references during the same period to the severity of his depression; they also ignore the general clinical pattern of depression that allows for "breaks" that bring a temporary reversion to "normalcy"—before the sufferer (often suddenly) reverts to depression's more typical bleakness. All the dissenters from the verdict of suicide assume that the thoughtful and restrained person whom they knew as Primo Levi and whom some of them had encountered as that person in conversations or correspondence shortly before his death would not soon afterward throw himself headfirst down the stairwell of Corso Re Umberto 75.

But this pleading hardly warrants the conclusion drawn from it, even without the counterevidence mentioned. Was suicide to be as thoughtful or reasoned an act as those the person—any person—"normally" performed? The requirement itself is unreasonable. And then, too, of course, to reject the verdict of suicide leaves untouched the question of how Levi *did* die. The principal, seemingly the only possible response to that question must then be to ascribe Levi's end to accident or misadventure: leaning on or over the banister near the stairwell and becoming disoriented, perhaps dizzied by his anti-depression medication, he fell over it. This version of the sequence cannot be ruled out, but physical probabilities argue against it. Levi was slight, about five-foot-five; the banister on the landing was a bit more than three feet high, reaching at least to his waist—a combination of numbers that makes an accidental fall, with Levi faint or unconscious or at any rate unable to control his balance, unlikely. But then, too, the possibility has been posed that perhaps he was walking down or back up the stairs, past an area where the banister was lower than on the landing, and *then* fell over it. Again, the possibility cannot be excluded, although additional explanation would be needed of why Levi, against his custom of using the elevator, had been walking up or down the stairs. And the pressure remains of how to weigh those possible accounts against the other factors already mentioned as likely contributors to his suicide, none of them conjectures, as the others are, about Levi's movements after he received his mail that morning from the concierge (the last person outside the apartment to see him alive) or about the differing heights of the banister or about the difficulty he "must" have foreseen in planning a jump through the narrow aperture of the circular staircase. What is certain beyond these conjectures is that Levi did die from a fall and that there are reasons for inferring that the fall was deliberate. And if not deliberate in the sense of reasoned, at least as having been initiated by him.

Additional circumstantial factors supporting this claim surface from unexpected directions. So, for example, suicide had been a presence not only in Levi's awareness of history but in his personal relations. His own family's past included the suicides of his paternal grandfather, Michele Levi, and a maternal uncle, Enrico Sacerdote. And there were others among his own acquaintances: Agostino Neri (d. 1938), a laboratory classmate in their second year at the university; the writer Cesare Pavese (d. 1950, in Turin), who as managing editor of Einaudi concurred in the publisher's initial rejection of *If This Is a Man* (and who was teaching at the elementary school in which Levi was a pupil, though not as Levi's teacher); Lorenzo Perrone (d. 1952), the Italian laborer at Auschwitz who risked his life to provide food for Levi but who on his own return to Italy destroyed himself (not in a single act but over several years—in Levi's words, "To live no longer interested him"; Levi would name both his daughter and son after him);[6] Hanns Engert (d. 1981), Levi's teacher of German at Turin's Goethe Institute where Levi enrolled in 1978 and with whom he built a personal friendship.

There were still other acquaintance-suicides, and then too, there were the public figures whose deaths affected Levi as incorporating histories which, like his own, the Nazis forced on them: Paul Celan (d. 1970), whose difficult postwar poetry Levi regarded as heralding his suicide, with the two "acts" traceable as deriving from a common source. And more, even *most* important for him, Jean Améry (d. 1978), whose accusation against Levi as a "forgiver" of the Germans stung Levi into denial but who also impressed Levi with his analysis of the condition of the "intellectual" in the camps, his account of being tortured as a Nazi captive, and his reflections on suicide, which came close to Levi's own view (Levi addressed these issues in a full chapter of his last book, *The Drowned and the Saved*).

Levi had himself noted what he took to be the infrequency of suicide in the Lager as well as in the ghettoes, as the Warsaw diarist Chaim Kaplan had claimed, countering the expectation that hardships suffered in those settings *would* conduce to suicide. No, Levi insisted—agreeing here with Améry that suicide assumes sufficient freedom to allow a person to step back and consider whether he or she wishes to continue to live (Améry emphasizes the difference between *Selbstmord*, "self-murder," the common German term, and *Freitod*, "free [voluntary] death," the term that Améry prefers).[7] In Levi's view, the Lager, in which demands of survival consumed all energy and thought, left no space for a Freitod.[8] When all human resources were exhausted, only the condition of the "Muselmann" remained—a final stage of life for "the submerged," as Levi represented it, where individuals became incapable of making decisions at all, including the decision to put an end to their own suffering.

How could Levi's conception of suicide as a Freitod account for his own last days? His sense of irony might have recognized that even his own act need not conform to his speculation, that suicide although at times voluntary might also at times be involuntary or nonvoluntary. And then, too, it is not clear, and cannot be, that he himself did not choose to do what he did, with background evidence in support of that. In his last months, he mentioned the possibility of suicide to a number of friends, as he also had even earlier. In 1982, in the trough of a depression, he had said to a woman confidante with a touch of bravado that in retrospect seems only grim irony: "I want to end it. But the third floor is not high enough."[9] In what we *know* about Levi's end, we find a virtual consensus among those closest to him: Lucia, his two children, his sister, and close friends who had known him for upward of fifty years including the jurist Bianca Giudetti Serra, Alberto Salmoni, and Silvio Ortona. For them, his last weeks with its depression and the numerous factors contributing to it as these together were viewed and measured against the background of years of intimacy led to only one conclusion, that what occurred was indeed suicide. This was also the judgment of a physiotherapist and a psychiatrist whom Levi had recently consulted professionally and who, basing their conclusions on their sessions with him, not only concurred with but insisted upon it.

Again, none of these reports, singly or collectively, is conclusive; given the circumstances as access to them is possible, nothing can be; even an eyewitness account, after all, would not fully settle the matter. But the available evidence is cumulative,[10] with a notable feature that those who find the balance of evidence going the other way were as a group farther removed from Levi than those in the other group—David Mendel, an English doctor who had only a short time before the death made Levi's acquaintance through correspondence and telephone (and one meeting) and who was oddly motivated at first to contact Levi in order to compose beforehand Levi's obituary; the novelist Ferdinando Camon, who met Levi in 1982 and then interviewed him, with Levi then checking Camon's account of their conversations in May 1986 before Camon's book was published (as mentioned, Camon received a letter from Levi after his death which referred to plans for the future; there is no reference in Camon's memoir to the matter of Levi's depression); the Oxford sociologist Diego Gambetta, who was not personally close to Levi but who could conclude in the *Boston Review* in 1999 from no more than the information cited here that "suicide is, at the very least, no more likely than an accident."

But again, neither personal relationship nor independent analysis can fully settle the issue, although each item of evidence may add to or subtract from a conclusion in different measures. Obviously, Auschwitz *together* with the factors mentioned would have been sufficient reason; but the assembly of factors *without* Auschwitz would also by such common standards as apply have sufficed—and indeed, the concept of sufficient cause in relation to suicide is intrinsically problematic, with the magnitude of alleged causes varying widely. Foregrounding Auschwitz as *the* cause or even as decisive among others, furthermore, assumes that the suicide rate among camp survivors is more to be expected—higher—than in other groups. But statistics related to that claim are scanty and at best inconclusive; however plausible the prima facie hypothesis that the specter of the camps would "naturally" add weight to the debility of aging, a parallel claim could be made for its contradictory—that the will to live that had once strengthened those who survived might also better enable them to withstand the new challenge of aging and illness. And of course, even if statistics did demonstrate a higher suicide rate among camp survivors, that would not determine its occurrence in this (or any) particular instance. Finally, then, doubts about the claim for Auschwitz as responsible for Levi's suicide run up against one question, both specific and broad: On what evidence does the conclusion rest other than the fact that Levi had in fact *been* there?

To assert the causal connection to Auschwitz as decisive, furthermore, erases the forty-two full years of Levi's life after his return to Turin from the Lager. Those years included his marriage—momentous, in his recollection: his "first woman"—and the two children born in it to whom he was deeply attached. He enjoyed an unusually large number of personal friendships and considerable professional success as a chemist and industrial administrator, the latter culminating in his advance to administrative head of the SIVA (Società industriale vernici e affini) plant where he worked. He had conveyed the spoken message of a witness-survivor to an increasingly large audience of schoolchildren and others in Italy, and through his published and personal writings to readers and correspondents worldwide. In 1978, soon after Améry's suicide, he articulated what amounts to the substantial difference that he found between Améry and himself: "Faced by his death, I have felt how fortunate *I* have been, not only in recovering my family and my country, but also in succeeding to weave around me a 'painted veil' made of family affections, friendships, travel, writing, and even chemistry."[11]

At the time of his death, Levi had achieved international recognition as a *writer*—recognition that although initially evoked by his accounts of the Lager, reflected also a body of work in short stories, essays, novels, and poems that had no connection to the Holocaust and that stood imaginatively and forcefully on their own. This acclaim for Levi as writer reached a level matched by few contemporary authors associated with *any* subjects—including the considerable number of Holocaust survivor-authors who focused on that event. Among the latter, Nelly Sachs had won the Nobel Prize for Literature in 1966; Imre Kertész, whose work reached beyond Hungary only after

Levi's death, would win the Nobel Prize in 2002; Levi was himself a candidate for the prize before his death and would undoubtedly have been a stronger one still had he lived. Arguably the one survivor-author of comparable literary stature during Levi's lifetime was Paul Celan, whose standing as a poet also reflected much more in his work than only the role of the Holocaust. The recognition accorded Levi, the prizes, the translations of his books into the major languages, and the many other honors and invitations he received gratified him; if the demands accompanying them also weighed on him, these collectively emphasize that whatever his last act was, Levi's death demarcated a life that did not end at Auschwitz metaphorically any more than it did literally.

Then too, beyond the doubts shadowing his death, a more basic question shadows *them:* Why should Levi's suicide, in fact or possibility, loom so large in thinking and speaking about him—continuing now, twenty-five years after his death and for many readers who encounter him first only in his posthumous appearance. Why? Does the matter of suicide alter the reach or meaning of his writings? The words and sentences, descriptions and reflections of his writings remain exactly as they would however he had died: the same images of the Lager, the same challenge to those who would obscure or deny its existence, the same—for some of his critics, cold—reflective eye with which he attempted to understand how the Nazis came to imagine and then implement their "Final Solution of the Jewish Question." And also, it should again be recalled, the same profusion of writings in which his experience of the Nazi years goes unmentioned, where themes of nature's ingenuity and human irony are at once his subject and his means. All these exhibit a remarkable grasp in mind and imagination of the intricacies of nature's nature and of the power of thinking itself.

Some of his readers have argued that to accept the verdict of Levi's suicide projects backward a shadow on his writing as well as on his life—that it *does* alter his texts. But determinist or biographical readings of literary texts, like all "intentional" explanations, bring with them their own problems; in the end, whether readers want to know it or not, they have to trust the tale, not the teller. That is, unless they are willing to substitute their imagination for the author's, the effect of which is to give up on reading altogether. Some critics in this group have claimed that the act of suicide would undo the intellectual and emotional strength credited to Levi as survivor and witness. But *why?* Physicians fall ill without reversing the cures effected earlier, certainly without being guilty of malpractice; someone who breaks one promise does not nullify others made before or after that one, still less those that the person had made good on; military withdrawals are not always marks of defeat, still less so of cowardice. And these analogies are themselves relevant only as one already assumes a problematic moral status for the act of suicide. If foreshadowing appears at all in Levi's writing, a more notable tell-tale would be his optimism that reason and method can find their way through anything not intrinsically impenetrable—a claim on the future that was for him unaltered by suicide as a phenomenon whenever it occurred and that would remain undiminished, one might assume, even with his own. Does the manner of Levi's death in any way alter Levi's startling characterization of his writing when he notes that if he were to reconstruct his own literary genealogy, it would be *Rabelais*, that source of exuberant and boundless laughter in the midst of darkness, whom he would choose as his literary father?

That the "question" of his suicide is often the first topic raised in discussions of Levi is not unique to his life and writing, and this more general reaction underscores the specific issue of his death. For the relation between death deliberately chosen, on the one hand, and art in *its* deliberations, on the other, has obtruded on the reading of authors as different from one another as Sylvia Plath and Vladimir Mayakovski, Hart Crane and Ernest Hemingway, John Berryman and Cesare Pavese, with the interest in their deaths surfacing for them all with repetitive questions, inferences, innuendos. Suicide may seem to add drama to the lives of already dramatic figures; perhaps it does this with more intensity for writers and artists than for others just because their work *gives* life to events and qualities that otherwise appear inert or silent. But whether their personal "ends"—deaths—retroactively alter their creations and as a consequence of that force revision in the readings of their work carries an unmet burden of proof. Are all readings prior to their authors' suicides which did not (because they could not) take that end into account nullified? Is a writer's death itself also part of the written creations? Should readers be expected to suspend responses to the work of artists about whose lives (and deaths) they know little until they know more?

Imagine a scenario of counter-history for Primo Levi's end: that Levi died not from a fall, but from a heart attack, suffered as he walked into his apartment building on April 11, 1987, collapsing then in the stairwell. Would *that* "end" make a difference to what readers find in his writings or alter Levi's meaning for them? Would it make *any* difference beyond its contrast with what did happen, or would it even touch the extremity to which human desperation can lead—itself known well from so many other sources, including Levi's own writings? For those who insist that Auschwitz defined everything that followed in Levi's life, even the heart attack might only confirm the pattern: stress from the Lager was exacting its toll forty years later. Of course, the same argument could be applied if Levi were to have died at the age of ninety (just a few years ago; as life expectancies go, he might be alive even now)—as it might also if his sudden death had occurred even before his actual one, in an automobile accident or by murder. Some of the reasoning here is straightforward: his family history was of cancer (father) and

Residents of Corso Re Umberto 75.

aging (mother); since death by suicide is not usually counted among "natural causes," the inference then goes that there must be an irregular reason for this irregularity in the hereditary pattern. And since among the known irregularities in his lifetime, Auschwitz is *very* irregular, ergo . . .

But this reasoning raises more questions than it resolves. Nothing in it changes the illumination Levi provided for those to whom he spoke when alive and continues to speak in death: the remarkable grasp of mind and language, the intelligence and the creative pleasures of a searching imagination. And his great, enduring patience in the face of facts and the matter they embody—even when at a certain point those facts and matter force his inheritors (us) to recognize that even his great patience and persistence had limits, that although they carried him farther than other people could imagine on their own, there was a point beyond which he too could or would not go. *These* qualities seem more revealing of Primo Levi and more responsive to what he said and wrote than whatever is known or remains in question about his "end." For those who begin thinking about Levi from the last point in his life backward and still more for those who begin elsewhere, his end leaves everything else unaltered and, still more certainly, undiminished. Even as an ending, it demands to be understood as a beginning, with all the reasons for that entry provided first by Levi himself.

2

The War

FORTY YEARS after the event, Levi was "astonished" at the
summer excursion in August 1943 that he and his sister and
friends took to the Piedmont mountain town of Cogne. Forty
years after that—*now*, 2013—the excursion still seems improbable. At the time of Levi's holiday, World War II had reached
its "world" extent. Six months earlier, the Battle of Stalingrad
ended in Germany's surrender with a total number of about
two million dead in the eight-month struggle. By August, after
almost two years of fighting in the Pacific and North Africa,
the United States had suffered 50 percent of its total wartime

casualties. Units of the German and Italian forces that in May had surrendered to the Allies in North Africa were fighting in Sicily, where the Allies had landed on July 10.

This news on a large scale stood side by side with events closer to home for Levi. The Allied bombing of Italy, from north to south, was intensifying, and he had himself experienced it. His group left Milan for their August holiday during a heavy air raid, and he returned to find the building in which he roomed uninhabitable; his home city of Turin had been bombed first in June 1940 and with increasing frequency afterward, and the growing frequency reflected the turning tide of the war. In addition, by August 1943, more than two-thirds of the six million Jews murdered in the Holocaust were dead. The six main killing camps—the death factories epitomizing the "Final Solution of the Jewish Question"—had been active since July 1942; three of them (Belzec, Sobibor, and Treblinka) would *cease* their murder operations in the two months following Levi's summer excursion. Then, too, in the five months after August 1943, Levi would become a member of a partisan group in the Piedmont mountains, endure capture by Italian Fascists and transfer to a collection camp at Fossoli, be packed at Carpi into a freight car sent on its way to Auschwitz, and then find himself *there*. A prediction of this future in that same August would undoubtedly have produced greater incredulity in Levi at the time even than his reaction to his summer excursion forty years later.

At the time, moreover, Levi's carefree attitude about the war was plausible as well as possible. The 1938 racial laws imposed in Mussolini's Italy—Mussolini's since 1922—were the first specifically exclusionary laws affecting Italy's Jews (the 1929 Lateran Treaties, arguably a foreshadowing, had established Catholicism as the state religion), and even the 1938 legislation did not revoke the Jews' citizenship as the Nuremberg Laws had mandated for German Jews three years earlier. The

definition in the Italian racial laws of who was Jewish was also
more limited, requiring as a minimum one Jewish parent (the
father)—and even then parents and children were excluded
from the category if they had converted in time (October 1938);[1]
this in contrast to the requirement of three Jewish *birth* grand-
parents that with a few variations had been mandated in Germany under the definition attached to the 1935 Nuremberg
Laws. Partly because of its relatively small numbers (48,000
in the 1938 census); partly because of the community's acculturation and economic status; partly because of the Catholic
Church's traditional ambivalence toward Jews—at once stig-
matizing them and willing their preservation *as* stigmatized—
and partly because of the casual attitude more generally in Italy
toward group discrimination, the Jewish community had not
only sustained itself but flourished with little social or political hindrance since the country's unification in 1861 (its full extent came in 1870), despite occasional outbursts of stereotypi-
cal antisemitism. Various indicators of Italian Jews' public roles
reflect this. Although they made up less than 1 percent of the
populace, more than 15 percent of the Senate in 1920 was Jewish; the Italian armed forces in World War I included 50 Jewish
generals—and an estimated 230 Italian Jews participated in the
march on Rome in October 1922 that later came to symbolize
Mussolini's rise to power. Nor, given these appearances, was
it surprising that the Italian-Jewish middle and upper class—a
substantial portion of the community—would largely support
Mussolini and the promise he represented to them of social
stability. (They also provided some of the early opposition to
Mussolini through the Communist and Socialist Parties, but
that opposition became a serious political factor only later in
the war years.) When the 1938 anti-Jewish racial legislation was
passed, it is estimated that about a third of the adult Italian-
Jewish populace—about 10,000—were members of the Fascist
Party; Cesare Levi, Primo's father, was among them. The 1938

legislation forced these Jewish members out of the Party, but even after that happened, many of the same group remained both regretful and hopeful. Primo Levi recalls his father speaking optimistically at the time about the future: "Ah, but we're in Italy. . . . They wouldn't dare do anything to us."[2]

The same 1938 legislation also prohibited the enrollment of Jews in "mixed" educational institutions, a rule that would have ended Primo Levi's days at the University of Turin, which he entered in 1937, had it not been for a clause in it which permitted Jewish students in their second university year or beyond that to complete their degrees. Levi was thus able to continue his studies, and he then received his degree in chemistry in 1941. During those student days, furthermore, he was permitted (and agreed) to join the Fascist club at the university—a membership, he commented, that allowed him access to facilities at the university that he would otherwise have been denied. (At the age of five, he had been one of the Sons of the Wolf—Figli di Lupa, roughly comparable to American Cub Scouts—the children's organization initiated by the Fascist government.) After receiving his university degree, he twice succeeded in finding employment as a chemist, although in order to obtain those positions his Jewish name and identity had to be disguised, a deception he managed with the complicity of his non-Jewish employers.

Until shortly after his August excursion, Levi's family and circle of friends in Turin and in Milan, where he was then working, provided a measure of insulation from events of the war outside Italy and to an extent within it. Even his initial involvement with street activities during that time—distributing opposition pamphlets, tearing down Fascist Party posters— though dangerous, had various buffers around it. The "abnormality" of being Jewish was certainly more constrictive than the position of the non-Jewish populace, including those who opposed fascism, but notable elements of increased suffering and hardship were common to the two groups. The costs of the war, the increasing damage to Italy's cities from Allied bombings, the casualties suffered by Italian forces fighting alongside the Germans, and a growing disillusionment with the tactics and justifications of Mussolini as leader—Il Duce—all those were shared. Then, too, there was the lurking issue in Italy, more than in most western European countries, of the sparse public information about what was not yet recognized or understood as "the Holocaust." Looking back, one of Levi's recollections mentioned in *If This Is a Man* seems much *more* than astonishing: when he and the others among the 650 Italian Jews in the transport taking them to Auschwitz saw a sign at the beginning of their journey at the rail siding in Carpi which indicated their destination as "Auschwitz," the name meant nothing to them. Their first thought was that it might be a variant or misprision of "Austerlitz"—a punning mistake on the site of the Napoleonic victory and the Paris railroad station.[3] Levi's recognition of Auschwitz for what it *was* thus began only when his transport arrived at the place itself on February 26, 1944. At that time, the gas chambers of Auschwitz, the consummation of the Nazis' search for an impersonal means of mass murder, had been in operation there for almost two years.

Although Primo Levi's personal declaration of war reached a decisive point before that arrival, it too came only after his group's summer excursion to the mountains in August 1943. Indeed, it was only then that news of the events unfolding in the countries occupied by Germany began to challenge the general incredulity at the piecemeal reports of the "Final Solution" that had previously begun to reach Italy. From the distance of 2013, the fact that such incredulity may itself seem incredible only underscores the temptations of historical hindsight and the widespread sense of disbelief in the abnormal that is so constant a feature of it. A defining instance of that incredulity occurred shortly before Levi's summer excursion, mainly because it was indeed a world apart from it—in the reaction to reports by Jan Karski, the Polish non-Jewish emissary who had slipped into the Warsaw Ghetto and the sorting camp at Izbica (preliminary to the death camp of Belzec) in order to obtain eyewitness evidence, and who then conveyed his eyewitness testimony first to the Polish Government in Exile and then to government officials among the Allies in London and Washington. In July 1943, Karski recounted these observations to a small group in Washington that included Felix Frankfurter, a Jewish U.S. Supreme Court justice and confidant of President Roosevelt. The details of Karski's report are known; in any event, he had no need to embellish or exaggerate what he heard in Frankfurter's courteous yet strained response, in terms that Frankfurter also later reported himself: "I do not say that you are lying but I don't believe you."[4]

The Allied invasion of Sicily and the tide of the war more generally precipitated Mussolini's deposition and arrest on July 25, 1943. He was succeeded as head of government by Marshal Pietro Badoglio, who after weeks of increasing pressure—reaching a critical point with the invasion of Italy's "toe" on September 3—negotiated Italy's surrender to the Allies on September 8. Badoglio attempted unsuccessfully to keep the surrender secret; the Germans quickly took open control of the areas in which they were already present, inclusively in the North and extending to principal cities, including Naples, in the South. The official Italian surrender had led many in the country to believe that for Italy at least the war was over, but the euphoria of this reaction was quickly punctured by the Germans' "rescue" of Mussolini from captivity on September 12, followed by their creation of a puppet government at Salo with Mussolini as its titular head and the increasingly harsh Nazi grip on the areas of Italy they controlled. This included severe actions against the hundreds of thousands of returning Italian soldiers who had been fighting alongside the Germans in Greece, in North Africa, and on the Russian front: those who refused to join the German military "voluntarily" were often sent to forced-labor camps in Germany; others were killed outright (Italian units on the island of Cephalonia who first resisted German authority and then surrendered were massacred). And Nazi control in Italy, in collaboration with the Italian Fascists, who took part more openly in this, brought a systematic increase in the roundups and deportation of Italian Jews, about eight thousand of whom—a sixth of the community—would eventually perish. The most widely known of these roundups occurred in Rome on October 16, "under the very windows" of the Vatican.[5] That was followed by the deportation of more than a thousand of the number seized, who within a week would find themselves in Auschwitz; of that group, fewer than thirty survived the war. Levi and the others in his transport from the collecting camp of Fossoli arrived at Auschwitz four months after the October roundup; he had no way of knowing from the few Italian Jews he then encountered how many others had arrived before him.

In connection with Primo Levi's own war, October 1 is the date usually given for his joining the partisans (that date appears in the national records of the Resistance). His own group was small, varying in estimates between nine and fifteen members (eleven is the number he himself cites in his story "Gold" in *The Periodic Table*). Only three of the group had military training. Levi himself had none that could have made a difference; the Fascist Militia he was forced to join and to train with at the university had only wooden rifles to drill with; there is no evidence that he ever fired a real one. (The racial legislation of 1938 that allowed him to continue studying also forced him out of this university Militia group.) The term *joined* as applied to his partisan group is itself an exaggeration. Levi and his companions in effect set up their own group, although they modeled it on the "Justice and Liberty" partisans, some of whom were already active in the Piedmont mountains.

In addition to being untrained, Levi's group was ill-equipped; he refers in "Gold" to the small "lady's" pistol he had acquired that he never fired. But it was not only this amateurish quality and the group's harmless forays (aside from the seizure of one cache of arms in the mountains, their main efforts were directed at gathering food for themselves from nearby villages) that led Levi, who would later describe in close detail aspects of his months in Auschwitz, to write briefly and dismissively about his time as a partisan. The period as a whole, from October 1 to his early-morning capture by Italian Fascist units on December 13, saw Levi in a role entirely different from any he had previously had or imagined: a combatant. And although the village of Amay, where his group was quartered, was not immediately endangered and did not pose nearly the threats he later underwent and observed in Auschwitz, it is unlikely that Levi's eye for detail and the impulse to write about the unusual events he witnessed would not have been active then as well: the setting of the Piedmont mountains and its warring groups had enough complexity and enough peril to hold his attention. But Levi later would later say flatly and notably briefly that the period was "of no account, trivial." "My experience as a partisan counted very little. Very little. I was a partisan for a few months only, and in name only, since I wasn't even armed." As late as 1980 he would write to Paolo Momigliano, president of the Historical Institute of Resistance in Valle d'Aosta, that his time as a partisan was "without doubt the most opaque of my career, and I would not recount it willingly. . . . It's better among things forgotten."[6] And yet two and a half months as a partisan in that setting was not a negligible period in duration or stress; the reasons he gives for his reticence in discussing it suggest more than only the sense that nothing important occurred during that time—and there is ample evidence both that something important *did* occur and what it was.

Embarrassment at his group's or Levi's own ineffectuality might partly explain his avoidance, but a specific event was more directly relevant and was almost certainly of lasting significance for Levi. Details about the event are only hinted at in his own allusions to it, and even the fragmentary accounts provided by others who were at the scene, though more explicit than Levi's, remain incomplete. Taken as a whole, however, enough has been reported about the event to prove that feelings of shame and guilt are at least as pertinent to Levi's avoidance as embarrassment. The very intensity of the silence points to its being an occurrence as important for understanding his "war" as does the impassioned voice in his writings about other parts of that war.

The event itself is readily summarized: on the night of December 8, four days before what would be the group's capture, in Frumy, a village close to Amay, two members of the partisan group quartered there were shot—executed—by Sergeant-Major Berto of the partisans. That punishment was imposed because of what is described as a rampage in nearby St. Vincent—"drunken looting"—by the men executed. That summary is simple, but the punishment was anything but simple for the group and arguably least of all for Levi. Apparently, he did not participate in or witness the execution; it remains unknown what part he had in the decision to punish the two men in that way. Whatever his distance from it, however, he was sufficiently involved to feel responsible for an act that brought him as close as he would come in his role as a partisan to killing another human being. That the killing had as its victims two members of his own group would intensify his reaction immeasurably. Levi repeats elsewhere in his writings how deeply repellent he found *all* violence; he recognized the intensity of this feeling to the point of describing himself as "a coward" because of it. That the violence in this occurrence was directed not against the enemy, recognizable and close, but against their own ostensible partners underscored its difference from his group's combination of ineptitude and inaction—their own inadvertent nonviolence. Even for someone without Levi's sense of irony, this effect would have been emphatic; with it, the silence about the episode that he chose to maintain then and afterward must have required an unusual effort of will.

There were, to be sure, other topics that Levi also avoided; few writers are without such taboos, however varied the specific boundaries. And any attempt to interpret what Levi or other authors choose *not* to write about adds to the already substantial difficulties of interpreting what they *do* write. But Levi himself identifies certain topics that he avoids and his reasons for doing so; for example, his silence about familial relations which extended to his close, often covert friendships (largely, perhaps always nonsexual) with various women: "I prefer to keep quiet my sentimental relations for reasons of decency, discretion, and reserve."[7] But that principle could not explain avoiding the unusual event he conceals even in the brief accounts he provides of his history as a partisan. The fullest but still oblique reference he makes to that event is couched in terms that still leave the event itself obscure. Thus, in "Gold" in *The Periodic Table*, Levi writes of himself and the other partisans in prison just after their capture: "Among us, in each of our minds, weighed an ugly secret: the same secret that exposed us to capture, extinguishing in us, a few days before, all will to resist, indeed to live. We had been forced by our consciences to carry out a sentence and had carried it out. But we had come out of it destroyed, destitute, waiting for everything to finish and to be finished ourselves; but also wanting to see each other, to talk, to help each other exorcise that so recent memory."[8] The intensity of feeling recorded here is unmistakable, but its source remains unspoken and indeterminate. If not for accounts by others in the partisan group, nothing more would be known about that secret; these words by Levi and still vaguer references in two poems, "Epitaph" and "Partisan," are all that he has to say about the episode.[9] It remains an instance where the significance of the silence is proportionate to its extremity; understood in this way, his near-silence brings into what is at most a shadowy light certain radical contours of Levi's war that would otherwise remain in full darkness.

Levi's capture in the early-morning hours of December 13 by the Italian Fascist Militia followed the betrayal to the Militia of the group's location and resources by a member of the Fascists who pretended to join one of the partisan groups. The capture took place without a fight, although several of Levi's group were able to flee in the turmoil. Levi and three other members of his group were taken captive: Vanda Maestro, Luciana Nissim, and Aldo Piacenza (who had military training, having served in the Italian army on the Russian front). Those four, together with a fifth, Guido Bachi, who was captured as the others were being brought to the prison in Aosta, were interrogated there. That process would prove decisive for Levi in an unusual and unexpected way. When he joined the partisan group, he had obtained false identity papers with his family name listed as "Ferrero," resident of the Mezzogiorno and (by implication) not Jewish. But the façade of this false identity crumbled quickly after he was taken prisoner and even after he had eaten his identification card: one of his captors came from that region. With Levi's assumed identity useless, the Blackshirt officer interrogating him confronted Levi with a fateful choice.

In Levi's own report of this sequence, repeated with slight variations in his writings and in several interviews, the interrogating officer is described as having forced a choice of identity on him: "If you are a partisan, we'll put you up before the wall; if you're a Jew, we'll send you to Carpi [near the holding camp]." In the event, the consequences of the second alternative turned out to be radically different, and even the consequences of the first alternative were not those he had foretold: some of the non-Jewish partisans captured in the same operation were imprisoned and survived the war. But of course nothing of those outcomes could have been known to Levi at the time; in a single moment, he was forced to choose an identity, and he had no reason to doubt the terms of the choice presented to him. Initially, he rejected them both, claiming to be in Amay for skiing and hunting. But he soon gave that up, then considered the decision posed for him as if its alternatives were somehow evenly balanced, with the choice between them warranting deliberation. Finally he did decide. Levi would later write (not altogether convincingly): "Partly out of weariness, partly out of pride, I chose to be Jewish."[10]

Whatever Levi's fate would have been had he "chosen" to be a partisan rather than a Jew, it would surely not have brought him into the history that followed the choice he did make: no Fossoli, no Auschwitz, none of the writings about the Lager, few or even none of other topics that would later appear as his other writings. And of course, death itself might have followed: no future at all. If he had survived with a choice of his identity as a partisan, the only feature of the life he did go on to live that would probably have been unchanged was his career as a chemist and administrator. Given the educational and professional decisions he had made before joining the Resistance, only certain other unusual contingencies among history's normal contingencies would have altered that.

Brief as Levi's war was in his role of formal combatant, then, it turns out to have been much more consequential than he was later willing to acknowledge. And if the fashioning of one's own life history often reshapes that history "as it really was" because of personal remorse or distaste, this one event in Levi's war seems to have been and to have remained an unusually revealing example. Perhaps the period following it that

Levi spent in the internment camp at Fossoli provided a space in which he could distance himself from what had occurred; certainly that time, at least initially, was less tension-ridden than what had happened previously, to say nothing of what would occur afterward. The conditions Levi found at Fossoli when he arrived there on January 27 along with Vanda Maestro and Luciana Nissim were relatively benign. The camp itself at the time of his arrival was overseen by Italians; it included not only Jewish captives who had been rounded up in Italy but others who had been transported from Libya and Salonika. Some of the camp internees were non-Jews: British POWs, Yugoslav political prisoners. Those in the camp were allowed "family life" during the day, although men and women were separated at night. On one hand, the living space was constrained; on the other, there was no forced labor, and the food provided by camp authorities could be supplemented by packages from the outside. Mail brought news from the world, and early on visitors were permitted (not family members, who would also have been imprisoned, although a few managed to get through by using false identities). In the minds of both the Jewish captives and their Italian captors, however uncertain the future seemed otherwise, nothing imminent seemed more threatening to the Fossoli Jews than what they had experienced in being brought to the camp or in the conditions of life there.

All this changed sharply in mid-February, when S.S. officers and soldiers suddenly appeared in the camp and overtly took control from the Italian officials. The change proved a bitter development also in Primo Levi's own war, although it would be much more than that for most of the other Jews in the camp, who would be murdered soon afterward. Immediately, the Nazi officers altered the camp's informal procedures; more ominous, they announced that Jews in the camp were to be moved elsewhere. The internees had already understood in a general way the difference between Italians and Germans as captors;

in the presence of the Germans themselves, what they had heard previously—and managed to ignore or repress—about the treatment of Jews in the occupied countries now resurfaced concretely.

Levi's description in *If This Is a Man* of preparations on the day and night of February 21, before the journey that had been announced, reflects the grim atmosphere. He writes about the women in a group from Tripoli: "When all was ready, the food cooked, the bundles tied together, they unloosened their hair, took off their shoes, placed the Yahrzeit candles on the ground and lit them according to the customs of their fathers, and sat on the bare soil in a circle for the lamentations, praying and weeping all the night." (It is difficult to trace the sources of these customs; Yahrzeit candles are typically lit in the Ashkenazic—European—tradition in memory of those already dead.) In Levi's account, he is among a group of onlookers from the camp who also found the practice distinctive. Levi identifies the women as members of "Gattegno's" family: Italian Jews who had gone to Libya as workers when Italy took control of the country.[11]

Levi's deportation to Auschwitz occurred after he had been at Fossoli for slightly less than a month. On Levi's account, there seemed to be no sense among camp inmates that anything they might do could alter what was planned for them; he mentions no attempts (or thoughts of his own) to resist or to escape, although the latter would have been relatively easy— certainly easier than at any later time, although they could not have known that. The internees were taken by truck from Fossoli to the rail siding at Carpi, where a train waited. Any doubts about what they could expect after that were dispelled by the freight cars making up the train, the way in which the "passengers" were shoved into them, and the condition inside the cars that registered as they were locked up: 650 occupants in twelve cars, with Levi's car, smaller than the others, holding 45.

No provision had been made for toilets (why *would* there be in freight cars?); many on the transport had prepared food, which they carried with them, but few anticipated that water, which required no preparation or expense, should have been brought as well. The pressure in the indiscriminate assembly—infants and the aged, men and women, the healthy and ill—was intensified by the crowding; the conditions of physical pain and psychological humiliation could only increase. Once they were locked into the cars, the train stood in place for four hours; the journey of four nights and five days then began, carrying the "passengers" into their new world.

There is no record that anyone on the train was aware of the existence of the gas chambers that awaited most of them at their journey's end. And not to know about that was surely also not to imagine it. But the conditions of the journey—the crowding, the thirst and hunger, the cold, the noise, the lack of toilets—were ominous enough. Levi describes the nights as he lay close to a woman he had known in Turin "for years" but not well; they knew "little of each other." In fact the two knew each other better than that, and readers can only try to fit this literary "supplement," as with others, into the narrative progression. (How Levi stretches and contracts history in his writing is discussed further in the next chapter.) In the memoir itself, the woman remains nameless, but it is known that she was Vanda Maestro. The time she spent in Fossoli was more fraught for her than for him; she had attempted suicide after hearing the announcement of the impending transport. (She would later die in Auschwitz.) But Levi's account of their nights together on the transport focused on the journey, not on what occurred before or after. "Now in the hour of decision, we said to each other things that are never said among the living. We said farewell and it was short; everybody said farewell to life through his neighbor."[12] Here, as elsewhere in his writings, Levi, precise and vivid in his usual power of description, passes in silence over the detail of what he nonetheless wants his readers to know was intense but still indeterminate personal intimacy.

The arrival at Auschwitz five days later, on February 26, 1944, added violence and confusion to the humiliation and pain of the journey itself. A "selection" among the new arrivals took place immediately, and Levi estimates that five hundred of those on the train were sent to the gas chambers directly, without being registered as having "arrived" at Auschwitz. Those choices evidently were based on age (too young or too old), fitness, and, for pregnant women or women with children, those conditions alone—for both mothers and children. Together with the others who survived this initial screening, Levi was processed: shorn, showered, and then tattooed with the number on his left forearm that he would retain for life—174517. Also, as it would turn out, after death: the number is inscribed on his gravestone in the Jewish communal cemetery in Turin.[13]

For details of life in Auschwitz itself, in addition to the general works written about that camp whose name has become a metonymy for the death and concentration camps collectively we have Levi's own observations and writings, which contribute intensity as well as detail and angle: *If This Is a Man*, portions of subsequent books—*The Truce, The Periodic Table*, and *The Drowned and the Saved*—and numerous essays and interviews. Levi claimed that he remembered the events of his months in Auschwitz photographically, without loss or addition, and there is ample independent evidence of his remarkable memory. He undoubtedly applied that faculty with intensity in the setting of Auschwitz, but there is also no doubt, by Levi's own admission as well as from other evidence, that even in *If This Is a Man*, parts of which he had begun to "think" on the spot, he introduced changes in characters and events in the context (he himself argued, in behalf) of the narrative. Again, I say more about this aspect of his writing in the next chapter.

Levi's account of his eleven months in Auschwitz combines

a narrative of his own survival with general reflections on the "concentrationary" world. The various threads of this narrative reflect an unusual measure of detached reflection that Levi himself would later ascribe largely to his scientific training and commitment. It seems likely that this ability to distance himself even from the most extreme conditions in which he found himself also contributed to his survival, although he repeated often in his writings and interviews the *decisive* role that good fortune and chance (the Italian *fortuna* elides the two meanings) played in his—indeed, in *any* Jew's—survival in Auschwitz. His claim on this point is not a matter of modesty. Jews were brought to Auschwitz to die: in some instances they were expected to work first, but even then the final goal set for them was death. The "normal" diet for camp inmates would have ensured this ending even if nothing else had contributed; inmates were given between 1,300 and 1,700 calories a day, which represents a death sentence over a relatively short period of time—in the camp's own calculations, three months. (The higher number of calories, often cited as minimal for sustained survival—1,700— is the estimated daily amount required for a person lying in bed and doing nothing else: not at all the condition of the camp Häftlinge.) Chance and good fortune brought Levi a number of significant benefits. These included the food he received from an Italian laborer at the camp who also came from the Piedmont region: Lorenzo Perrone, who took the opportunity—and risk—of bringing Levi additional soup rations daily over a period of six months. The two men had met on a work detail, and without discussion or being asked, Perrone began to provide his help soon afterward; he also managed to send three letters from Levi (also at personal risk), rewritten in his own hand, to a non-Jewish friend of Levi's in Turin and even to receive and pass on the answers to Levi. In addition, there was the unlikely factor of Levi's degree in chemistry; drawing on that, he passed an oral examination given by "Dr. Pannwitz," the head of the chemical laboratory in the Monowitz-Buna subcamp of Auschwitz (Auschwitz-III) in which Levi had since June or July been part of the "Chemical Kommando." Levi's admission to the laboratory, which was intended to contribute to the production of synthetic rubber, meant that he was able to work indoors—an enormous benefit once winter set in. Levi was one of three out of eighty candidates who were chosen for the laboratory; most of those who volunteered for the positions had no qualifications for the work other than the assumption that it would be to their advantage. Buna never succeeded in producing any synthetic rubber; the laboratory itself was finally shut down, in effect without having begun, at the end of December as Auschwitz itself entered its last days.

Other "chance" factors contributing to Levi's survival included the close friendship he formed with Alberto Dalla Volta, also an Italian Jew, who was close in age to Levi, vigorous, and inventive in ways complementing Levi's own ingenuity—most of all, he was a friend in a setting where individual isolation and the war of "everyone against everyone else" was the norm (Levi notes repeatedly that the Lager's harsh conditions consistently worked against any sense of solidarity, not for it). But more fortuitous than even these other chance occurrences—because more improbable even among the other improbabilities—was Levi's falling ill with scarlet fever in the last days of Auschwitz. Because of that illness he was admitted to the camp infirmary. And because he was there when the Germans evacuated the camp, forcing all the Häftlinge well enough to walk to embark on the death march that ultimately brought the small number who survived its first stage, Gleiwitz, to Buchenwald or Mauthausen, Levi and others in the infirmary who could not even walk were simply left to fend for themselves; they alone, in a manner of speaking, were "free." (An estimated 80 percent of those who set out on the death march died on the way, including Levi's friend Alberto Dalla Volta.) Why Levi and the others remaining in the camp were not killed on the spot remained a mystery; the simplest explanation was that the German guards and staff were too preoccupied with saving themselves from the oncoming Russians to bother about them. And in fact, a number of those who survived in the camp were shot by Nazi squads otherwise unconnected to Auschwitz who passed by after the general evacuation and paused on their way.

Eight days after the Nazi officers and guards left the camp, Russian troops appeared—shocked and, as Levi describes it, both ashamed and embarrassed to discover the condition of the Lager's inmates who were still, if barely, alive. (The larger number of the dead lay where they had fallen, in that sense seeming less of a challenge.) The Russians quickly began efforts to sustain the camp survivors, setting up nursing facilities which were for Levi the beginning of his revival; he remained in the now-Russian infirmary for a month. Despite that care, many of the former Häftlinge died after the "liberation," either because they were already beyond help or because, unmonitored, they ate more food than their weakened systems could tolerate.

Although emphasizing the role of chance as decisive in his survival, Levi did recognize certain qualities of his own as having contributed to it. Among these were his general physical fitness when he arrived at the camp—as a student, he had been a mountain climber, a sport he later wrote about and one that he continued to enjoy almost until his last days—and his knowledge of German, however fragmentary at the time: he had taught himself through German chemistry texts used in his courses. (Levi emphasized repeatedly how important it was for survival in the Lager to be able to understand the language of commands, typically given in German or Polish.) His psychological constitution was also a positive factor, although Levi acknowledges this only indirectly: his ability to maintain a distance from what was happening around him, even *to* him, as it occurred. This distancing was no doubt heightened as he described his experiences after the fact, when he was writing *about* his experiences, but the ability would have been present earlier as well. Jean Améry wrote about the special vulnerability of "intellectuals" in the camps in an essay that Levi took seriously and addressed directly in his last book. Améry argued that aspects of psychological or reflective distancing—together with the practical inattention or ineptitude often accompanying it—proved a liability in the camp, but Levi did not completely agree with Améry on this. (Perhaps because of his practical training as a chemist, Levi suggests wryly in reference to his own survival, at least at that time he was probably not yet "that much of an intellectual.")

In his observations of life in the Lager, where the abnormal was the norm, with the shift to the one from the other occurring quickly and unpredictably, Levi's own compass and his eye for detail captured sharp, photograph-like images of practice and personality. Whether that eye was only in training or already advanced toward the role of fiction writer—or whether it reflected simply the precision sharpened in Levi's practice as a chemist—hardly matters. For Levi, even early on, there was no significant difference between those sources; the "two cultures," as C. P. Snow would later name the humanities and science, were never admitted by Levi as separate: there might be ignorance but not division between them. The memoir of Auschwitz provides many examples of their convergence for Levi, as for example in his notion of "useless violence," which he attaches to the broad question of why the Germans would add humiliation and torment when the final goal of murder was already fixed (he elaborates on this concept in *The Drowned and the Saved*, and I discuss it more fully in Chapter 5). What he means by "useless violence" is epitomized in a relatively benign incident in which an S.S. guard who, when Levi, desperately thirsty in his early days in Auschwitz, plucks an icicle from outside the window to suck on, strikes it from his hand. In response to Levi's question "Warum?" (Why?), the guard responds, "Hier ist kein warum" (Here there is no why)—itself unintelligible to someone for whom the intelligibility of nature, *all* nature, was a premise of his intellectual life.[14]

To be sure, Levi recognized that torment, even at times torture, might sometimes be rationalized on utilitarian grounds. But how is one to understand those practices when no such use seems to apply and when the forms of abuse themselves take on genuinely imaginative qualities of refinement? The examples he cites range from having a band made up of Jewish prisoners playing as the Jewish laborers were marched to and from their work assignments; the strict regulations imposed for making up beds that hardly warranted the name; the restrictions on possessions of the Häftlinge and how these had to be maintained; the interminable lineups and roll calls. Levi came to see these as parts of the process of dehumanization, although the question of why remained for him a mystery. He offers another remarkable example of the same phenomenon when Alex, a Kapo, accompanies him for his interview with Dr. Pannwitz for the position in the chemistry laboratory. On the way back from the interview, Alex rights himself when he loses his balance by grasping a greasy wire running alongside, and he then "naturally, thoughtlessly" wipes his hand on Levi's shirt. "I hold him responsible now and ever for this."[15] Levi lingers on this act more than on others whose consequences were much more severe physically; its relative triviality brings out the full force of what he means by "useless violence."

Levi's account of Auschwitz describes the camp as he saw it, and this comes out perhaps most notably in his rare and brief references to the gas chambers. Their presence is a constant shadow, and he speaks directly at times about "the gas," more fully about the selections, which were known to everyone as heralding the disappearance of those selected, with their subsequent fate also known. But the gas chambers themselves never appear, possibly because Levi himself never saw them (certainly not because he doubted their existence), possibly because their constant but indirect presence had a powerful effect of its own, possibly because he would have found it impossible to bring his characteristic understatement to bear on them. An arguably more dramatic example of that absence and of his use of understatement more generally appears as Levi describes standing among the assembled prisoners forced to watch the hanging of one of their fellows who had taken part in an attempt to blow up the crematoria. Levi relates the details of the hanging in stark, unemotive terms; still more graphically, Levi tells his reader in the context of that description that he had previously been forced to witness thirteen other hangings: thirteen hangings that he had not mentioned or described, and on which he did not elaborate even in this one-time reference to them.

Levi's war when he was in Auschwitz was, on one side, a continuing battle to stay alive, to survive. He makes clear his efforts toward that goal, the improbability of success, the constant threat of violence and death, and below that the continuous pain of hunger and weariness, the discomfort of smells and sounds, of sights that could not be avoided. Somehow, despite all that, Levi constructed for himself an insulation of distance required for understanding, attempting to see beyond the immediate phenomena to aspects otherwise buried under the urgency of the moment: every moment. The panoply of individual characters whom Levi introduces to his readers moves across a spectrum that combines improbability with plausibility (and with pain on both sides); so, for example, Steinlauf, the Jew who had won the Iron Cross fighting for Germany in World War I and who in Auschwitz insists on washing himself daily in dirty water without soap and drying himself with his jacket, encouraging Levi to follow him in this practice in order to prove to their captors that we "refuse our consent"; Elias, the dwarf who in normal society would have been—and, as he survived, would be—a psychopath, who nonetheless flourishes in the camp by a combination of physical strength and a willingness to violate even the minimal norms in the camp's flimsy fabric; Shlome, the Polish Jew who is astonished that Levi does not speak or understand Yiddish, whose own native language is Italian, yet who insists that he is Jewish; Pikolo—the young and able Alsatian Jew assigned that name and role as go-between to the camp staff with whom Levi felt sufficiently at ease to begin to teach him Italian by way of Dante's canto on Ulysses, which Levi recalls (with a few gaps) from memory; Henri, "eminently civilized and sane," a master of calculation involving the unusual triad of "organization, pity, and theft." Levi found it pleasant to talk to Henri, but commented, "I do not want to see him again."[16]

The effect of this manifold is a view of both a Jewish and a concentrationary universe: an unusual Jewish community reacting to the extreme conditions of the camp where they are held as Jews and conducting themselves only humanly, for better and worse. It is a world of discovery for Levi, moving always and at the same time in different directions. But since science itself depends on uncovering what is new and to that extent unpredictable, Levi in gathering these impressions seems as "normally" himself under the conditions of the Lager as the figures he describes.

The last S.S. guards fled Auschwitz under the Russian bombardment on the night of January 18, 1945; Levi had then survived almost eleven months in the camp.

For nine days, Levi and ten others in the infirmary's infection room fended for themselves, rooting in the remains of the camp: putting together a stove on which to cook, digging up the stores of potatoes in the ground. One of their group died during that time; others would die soon afterward, but not until the ninth day, when Russian troops arrived in Auschwitz. The Russians found Levi and the others in the infection room and moved them to what had been the central infirmary at Auschwitz; Levi would remain there a month. But of course, he had not yet returned home. That would take another eleven months after the Russians arrived at Auschwitz. The rendering of his war in its selected moments had begun to take shape even as he was engaged with it: experiencing it, on one side, and thinking it, on the other—even at the time committing himself to a continuation of the war by other means. Certainly there seemed to be more passion in Levi's subsequent writing than he was ever willing or perhaps even able to express day by day, face to face. Levi would write about the journey home in his second book, *The Truce;* but that book was published sixteen years after *If This Is a Man* and is quite different from it: differently posed, differently directed. He was well aware of the long interval between the two books, of the changes that his own history in that time—including the reception of his first book—had made for him in the writing: he had married and was the father of two children; he had advanced at the chemical plant, SIVA, and his first book had turned from his initial draft of fourteen typewritten pages to a full-length book and best seller in Italy with translations abroad. None of this history is mentioned or hinted at in *The Truce,* but the book conveys some sense of his survival as itself a triumph, even if that term was not and would not be one that he would himself have used.

The plot of *The Truce,* supplied by the framework of a journey from its beginning to its end, builds on the use of contingency and adventure: the stuff of the picaresque, in which an expectation of the future is assumed—an assumption entirely absent in Levi's earlier description of Auschwitz. No doubt the odd shape of the return journey readily invited the genre of the picaresque. The distance from Auschwitz to Turin could have been walked in less time than it took Levi to cover it by train (Lorenzo Perrone, the Italian workman who brought Levi the extra rations of soup, *did* walk it). But Levi spent a month of that time in the Russian infirmary in Auschwitz, four months waiting for transport in the assembly camp at Katowice in Poland, and two more months waiting at another by-station in Starye Dorogi, in the Soviet Union. Even when a train finally did set him on the journey homeward, it first traveled east rather than west, then south and eventually west, almost as if governed by chance, stopping and starting again, traversing in the process Romania, Hungary, Austria. But it did eventually reach Milan, from which Levi had left for his summer holiday in August 1943.

In retrospect, Levi presents his return journey as a setting for comic events and local color: making certain of food supplies, encountering people who suddenly appear and just as suddenly disappear, re-meeting them and then re-leaving them, and waiting: not so much with a longing for home, a longing that he mentions only once in the book, but for a train. It is as if in *The Truce* he left behind the deliberate and deliberated figure whom readers encountered in *If This Is a Man*. Arguably still more notable in *The Truce* is the absence of any but a single reference to Levi's own condition or emotion related to the return itself, the apprehension that would have seemed inevitable after what he had endured, and of any expression of anxiety over what he might find or not find "at home" when he did arrive there; after all, he had no way of knowing whether his mother or sister were even alive. Nor does Levi write about the approach or return to Turin after his train crossed the Italian border. Because of a gap in the train schedules, he stopped at a friend's home in Milan before traveling on to Turin—but he does not mention this in *The Truce*. (We learn from other sources that the Milan friend whom he visited told him that his mother and sister were indeed alive.)

And when Levi crossed the threshold of the family apartment at Corso Re Umberto 75, on October 19, 1945, other sources provide most of the details known about that reunion. We do hear from him, as well as from others, that he was barely recognizable to the concierge of the apartment building or to the friends who quickly assembled once they heard of his return. We hear from others about his eating for some time afterward always with a hand held under his mouth, as if to make certain that no food could escape—and of keeping bits of food in his pockets when he walked outside the house. Just in case. And we hear indirectly of Levi's resentment of those who had remained in Italy during the war but seemed unable or unwilling to take in what he was telling them, notwithstanding the harsh experience that many of them had had in their own survival, sometimes in the Resistance itself. It seemed to Levi that Auschwitz and what he endured and witnessed there were still so far outside their ken as to be unintelligible or unimaginable. There was no doubt, and he understood this, that atrocities and hardships for the Jews who remained in Italy were real and severe. But the concentrationary world would remain for him of a different order, and Levi found it difficult to comprehend that the accounts he provided of Auschwitz would be almost as difficult to conceive in the immediate aftermath of the war—even in his own presence—as Auschwitz itself had been in prospect.

The combination of shock and resentment that came with this realization did not make Levi's homecoming, his reentry, easier. What has come to be referred to as "overcoming [or 'mastering' or more neutrally 'confronting'] the past" in Germany and its allies and in countries occupied by the Axis has been more complex for Italy than most of the other countries for a variety of reasons and not only as related to persecution of the Jews. Italy was at once part of the Axis, a Fascist source, and outside it; even after the Badoglio "peace" treaty, Italians were fighting against Italians both on behalf of and against the Axis. It is estimated that more than 50 percent of the approximately eight thousand Italian Jews murdered in the war were victims of Italian Fascists, not the Germans. When to this is added the contentious role of the Catholic Church in Italy in relation to fascism before the war and then in relation to the Italian Jews during it—and to *that* the apologetic defensiveness and even denial common throughout the native populations of all European countries that had significant Nazi activists, the complexity of "overcoming the past" becomes still more evident than ever—and even if it has been late in coming, it certainly has increasingly become the subject of research and analysis.[17] (Perhaps the most notable, certainly one of the wittiest, statements heard in postwar Italy that might also serve as an exemplary motto of such apologetics was: "Non c'ero, e se c'ero, dormivo" [I was not there, and if I was there, I was asleep].)

Almost certainly related to this, Levi describes the quick compulsion that gripped him upon his return to speak of—to report on—the war he had seen and endured. He repeatedly compares that impulse to the need of Coleridge's Ancient Mariner to confront everyone he encountered with his account of the albatross he had killed. That urgency is the one principal aspect of his return that Levi does describe: the connection between that and his writing *If This Is a Man*, which would be the next step of his reentry. But why—the question is as imperative as its avoidance—does he *not* write about the return, his reception, and his reaction to it when he writes so fully about the lengthy journey to get home? To reach Turin and home had unquestionably been his goal, central to his longing in the Auschwitz months and then in waiting for the return; could it have been so much less so afterward in the return itself, when virtual silence ensues? Was it the impact of relief, the sense of a ponderous burden having been lifted, a burden so heavy that even when lifted it could make little difference, since his back

I. G. Farben complex at Monowitz-Buna (Auschwitz III), including the Buna laboratory.

was bent to its shape? Was it a sense of liberation inward as well as external—or that he was always readier to look outward, or at least to speak about external matters, than to look and speak inward? Levi would not have needed to tell his story to the other survivors who were also journeying homeward: each person's story was, roughly, everyone else's. And indeed since Levi was sent to the Lager without family, his arrival there set him off from many who survived with him but alone among their families. He did, as the train traveled steadily homeward, wonder about the "normal" people whom he saw in the countryside and in the stations they passed through: Munich, Vienna, Braunau (would he have been aware then that he was passing Hitler's birthplace?), Innsbruck. What had the people whom he now observed through the train windows known? What had they *done?* What did they now remember or think? But the train moved on, eventually finding its way to Milan. And then Levi went on to Turin.

Perhaps we are meant to conclude that when he reentered the apartment at Corso Re Umberto for the first time in more than two years, the weight of the moment was too heavy for words. And that it remained so even years later, when he found himself able to write about (almost) everything else. One thing we should not suppose is that when he stepped across that threshold, Primo Levi felt that his war had ended. For that would be to limit both *war* and *end* to their literal senses—which was not Levi's means of grasping them as he endured them, and would not be his means in remembering them. The Greek Jew Mordo Nahum, whom Levi served as a junior "business" partner as they waited together in the repatriation camp of Katowice, had been surprisingly unmoved when Levi reported to him on May 8 that the war was over; he replied only, "There is always war." Whether Levi agreed or disagreed with Nahum about that conclusion, it is certain that he remembered it. And he began writing.

3

Writing

"My 'perfect' reader . . . has with goodwill chosen
my books and would experience irritation or pain if he did
not understand line by line what I had written. . . . In fact
I write *for him* and not for the critics, nor for the
powerful of the earth, nor for myself."
—Primo Levi, *Other People's Trades*, 1989

"When someone asks me 'Why are you a chemist who
writes?,' I answer 'I write because I am a chemist.'"
—Primo Levi, *The Black Hole of Auschwitz*, 2005

"It's always dangerous transforming a
person into a character."
—Primo Levi, Interview with
Germaine Greer, 1985, in *The Voice of Memory*

W<small>HEN</small> P<small>RIMO</small> Levi died in 1987, he had published fourteen books—memoirs (or, as he preferred to call them, "autobiographies"), novels, poetry, collections of essays, short fictions. Parts of these had appeared earlier among the more than two hundred individual pieces he published in newspapers, journals, and anthologies: essays, short stories, poems, book reviews, prefaces. He had translated six books into Italian—from the French, English, German, and Dutch—and given about 250 interviews that were published or broadcast. Another novel, "The Double Bond," was nearly complete at the time of his death but remains unpublished. This oeuvre would be substantial by any standards and is a still larger accomplishment when one understands that Levi wrote much of it at the same time he was working full-time as a chemist and an administrator at the SIVA plant outside Turin that employed him for thirty years, from 1948 on.

But at the beginning: When Levi returned to Turin in October 1945, after the more than two years away that included his three months as a partisan, eleven months in Auschwitz, and the eleven months required for his return journey, he had published nothing and ventured only a few forays into writing. This contrast with his eventual achievement as a writer is not surprising, however, since his occasional writings during his university days and the several years after came about in part because that was what was "done" in his circle; there is no indication that he had considered in any serious way publishing what he wrote, much less turning to writing as a profession. When he began work as a chemist at the end of 1941, six months after receiving his degree at the University of Turin— much of that interval spent seeking a job—his career course seemed clear. His interest in chemistry and science had surfaced early in his schooldays at the *liceo*, where he already began to perform experiments outside the classroom; when he turned sixteen, he announced to his father the decision that he would be a chemist. That interest intensified and flourished at the university, where he received his degree in chemistry with highest honors accompanied by expressions of special approbation from his examiners. These accomplishments came despite the grip of fascism and the anti-Jewish racial legislation inside as well as outside the university; the announcement of his honors degree took care to mention that the graduate, Primo Michele Levi, was a "member of the Jewish race." Despite the law's additional prohibition of Jewish employment in non-Jewish firms, Levi, after his graduation and with the complicity of non-Jewish employers, managed to obtain two positions in chemistry. It was in 1943 while working near Milan at the second of those jobs—an eccentrically designed search for a drug to cure diabetes—that his life was "interrupted" in the radical way that also reshaped the career on which he had determinedly set out.

THE DIVIDED ROAD

Given the other events of Levi's war described in Chapter 2, to speak of his "war" as having "interrupted" his career is an obvious understatement. But having survived those events and returned to Turin, he was borne by the combination of his earlier education and his wartime memories into what was also the transformed life of home and career in postwar, non-Fascist Italy. For Levi this prospect became more trying than it would in any event have been because of the unexpected appearance of a fork in what had previously seemed the straightforward road of his career—his sustained interest in chemistry and training as a chemist. But that was now joined (more precisely, divided) by an impulse to speak and to write, and to do these about a subject which on its surface had nothing at all to do with chemistry. This was his experience *in* the war: what had happened to him, what he had seen happening, and, still more urgently in a reflective mind, what had *happened.* That second and divergent impulse came to evolve in its own pattern, eventually leading him also to subjects that had nothing to do with his war. But as a second "profession," it waited for years before he recognized it as anything like the formal profession of chemist with which he had much earlier identified. When he first began to write in the spare time left from his working days as a chemist, Levi followed the two forks of the road simultaneously, with a commitment to each and with a growing sense of gratification in accomplishment from each.

Soon after his return to Turin, he began looking for work as a chemist. After finding and leaving two other positions, in 1948 he joined SIVA (Società industriale vernici e affini), a then relatively small chemical business specializing in paints and varnishes. He later characterized his role at SIVA—indeed, he subsequently defined this one of his two professional roles—as "technician" not "scientist," distinguishing in this way between the scientist's emphasis on pure research and his own focus on the applications and problem-solving involved in the production of chemicals. He rarely spoke about the difference that this distinction made, but it clearly was significant since it represented for him both a basic career shift and a change that he saw as a direct consequence of his wartime experience. He described this change explicitly in a 1986 interview when, after taking Philip Roth on a tour of the SIVA plant from which he had retired a decade earlier, Levi responded to a question by Roth about his "scientific" role there: "I am not a scientist, nor have I ever been. I did want to become one, but war and the camp prevented me. I had to limit myself to being a technician throughout my professional life."[1] Even allowing for his modesty, Levi's recollection here reflects the actual distance between his work at SIVA and his student-day aspirations, when the laboratory, pleasurable as its practical work was to him (he repeatedly mentions the attraction to the senses—

sight, touch, smell—of the laboratory), seemed nonetheless a station on the way to the higher mysteries of theory. The Roth interview also brought up the unusual parallel between Levi and two other authors who combined careers of writing with employment in paint factories—Sherwood Anderson and Italo Svevo—although neither of them was a scientist (or much of a technician) in Levi's understanding of the terms.

In addition to the "war and the camp" as factors in his shift of profession to technician, economic considerations also exerted pressure. Levi's father, Cesare, had died of cancer in 1942 at the age of sixty-four, and when Levi returned to Turin, in addition to the need to support himself, he had also to consider the welfare of his mother and sister. And then, too, in 1947, he and Lucia Morpurgo were married—and the additional responsibilities this brought increased again a year later with the birth of their daughter, Lisa. Job openings were fewer for theoretical research in chemistry in postwar Italy than for commercial employment; the combination of need and opportunity pointed Levi in the direction of industrial chemistry. Levi's employment at SIVA provided a modest salary, but he found both the setting and the work there congenial. The head of the firm, Federico Accati, was an entrepreneur who recognized Levi's abilities, quickly giving him more responsibility than was usual. And the challenge on the job of the practical problems themselves engaged Levi's alertness to both the order and quirkiness of nature: the questions of how to satisfy requests by customers for novel, at times still imaginary products—as well as by others demanding to know why certain chemicals or products that SIVA had sold them were acting in unexpected and damaging ways. Such questions focused initially on varnishes and paints, but subsequently moved on, as the business itself did, to wire coatings, still as functions of their diverse, sometimes contradictory applications—as in demands for wire coatings, on the one hand, that would retain heat and for others, in contrast, that would inhibit or disperse it. Over time, Levi was himself recognized as a leading expert on issues related to wire coatings.

Such issues stirred—and connected—Levi's passion for demonstrating nature's orderliness and the inventiveness of his practical imagination. The attraction they had for Levi and his ability to work through them suggests that Levi would have had a successful career as a *criminal* detective, an analogy he himself once proposed. (In a stray aside, he mentions that if in a strange—presumably Italian—town you wanted to find a bar, you should look for a trail of chewing gum, since bar regulars spit out their gum before going in: an unusual application of the scientific method.) In any event, there was never any doubt about his skill as a *chemical* detective or the pleasure he found in its challenges, from problem-solving about the mottled surface produced by a particular batch of paint to what he saw as the adventures—odysseys in their own right—of the basic chemical elements that he came to characterize as the building blocks not only of chemistry but of nature itself. The possibilities of intrigue in this practice were undoubtedly a good part of what kept him at SIVA; even his subsequent promotion there and the increasing administrative responsibilities that came with it did not deter him, despite his impatience with some of his new work. Among other things, this later role required business travel for the firm, much of it involving visits to Germany. Aware of his wartime history and the fact that Levi was at least initially the sole Jewish employee at SIVA, the owner Accati was at first doubtful about asking Levi to undertake such contacts. But the same detached curiosity that Levi maintained during his captivity motivated him after it as well: his efforts to *understand* Germany in its Nazi project never left him, and in contrast to many survivors of the camps, especially in the early postwar years, Levi returned to Germany willingly. By his own estimate, he would eventually make at least fifteen business trips to Germany.

THE WAY TO WRITING

How, then, can we understand Levi's turn to writing? What brought his second and later profession to life? The shift or at least the divide in his conception of what he was and what he wanted to do is unmistakable. But in its origin and early history, this change was by his own estimate not an occupational transformation, certainly not a change in professions and not even the addition of a second one to the first. His student writings, as has been suggested, were for him a phase rather than the preface to a calling ("We were all writing poetry," he remembered). Indeed, so far as Levi came to think of writing as a profession (that is, as *his* profession), the shift occurred much later; the idea seems to have become explicit only after the publication of his second book, *The Truce*, in 1963—sixteen years after *If This Is a Man* appeared—and even then only tentatively, as though he were waiting still for fuller confirmation. This may seem an odd deferral for a writer who would eventually achieve Levi's commanding literary presence, but the evidence, external and through his own accounts, shows precisely this protracted development.

Levi repeatedly describes the origins of *If This Is a Man*—his account of his months as a partisan, his capture, and his deportation and eleven months in Auschwitz—as unmotivated by any ideal related to the art of writing or literary design. His description of that book's origin brings it closer to an eruption than to a decision at all: an expression which he felt *had* to come out and which appeared when it then did without deliberation or art: "almost spontaneously" and in any event, "with no literary intentions." Although he would eventually rearrange the book's chapters from the order in which they were initially written, after his rearrangement, they still did not follow a strict chronological order or other template; they seemed to continue to reflect the same "urgency" that the project had for him initially. "If there is literature there, it is unwanted, an intrusion. I certainly never considered problems of style." Or again: "In writing [*If This Is a Man*] I had no literary ambitions; I didn't set out to write a book, much less to become a writer." Even in the book's final (Italian) version of 1985, the chapters remain unnumbered: the matter of sequence, notwithstanding its post-liberation conclusion, may not be irrelevant for readers, but it seemed of lesser importance to Levi than the characterizations and reports of what he had seen and experienced.[2]

The act of writing that came in the aftermath of his release from Auschwitz was an attempt to describe his months there whenever and wherever he found an audience—motivated in no small part by his uncertainty that there would be an audience at all, at least any for which what he said would be credible. The image of Coleridge's Ancient Mariner recurs in Levi's account of himself during this postwar period and would persist long afterward: the drive to relate to anyone he encountered, stranger or friend, what had been so long bottled up. As an archetype of this sort, the Ancient Mariner raises an issue that Levi does not address directly: the *guilt* that in the Coleridge poem motivated the Ancient Mariner's testimony, but which if it figured at all in Levi's urgency came at a further remove. He does refer to the phenomenon of guilt reported by many survivors in relation to the others who had not survived that is stirred by the inadequacy of any explanation of why they had survived and the larger number of others had not. But as with much else in Levi's reflections on the Lager, his account of this too took an unusual form. Admitting to feeling some guilt for not having done more to help others, a larger source of guilt, he reported, stemmed from his consciousness of being a member of the same species capable of committing the acts for which the Nazis had been responsible—that there was at least this basic bond and a compelling one. That remarkable version of "survivor guilt" would thus apply to *everyone* living after Auschwitz, whether they had endured the war or not and whether they had been in the Lager or not. (Levi's conclusion here underscores the difficulties of defining the term *survivor* itself, which occurs in a range extending from those who had survived the death camps to those who while initially in harm's way had escaped to safe havens before the "Final Solution" began to be implemented.)

That Levi's impulse to recount his experience had found no earlier means of expression is understandable. In the Lager itself, there would have been no point to "reporting" or even talking about it; his fellow prisoners were experiencing the same menace and hardships, and there was in any event scant opportunity for speaking of it even if the Häftlinge wished to. The camp's isolation, furthermore, made it impossible to talk to anyone outside, and it was virtually impossible to speak to oneself by keeping a diary or journal: the very act of writing was a serious offense, even if paper and pencil could have been found. (Few diaries have survived from the concentration camps and virtually none from the death camps; the basic distinction between diaries and memoirs becomes significant as a consequence of this.) After the liberation of Auschwitz, Levi still found himself among survivors, and the imperatives of regaining his strength and arranging his return to Turin would preoccupy him—together, of course, with adjusting psychologically to the escape from the certain death sentence that had confronted him daily over an eleven-month period. Even when Auschwitz was still Auschwitz and Levi himself a Häftling, he knew that he wanted to, *had* to, bring word of the concentrationary world to those outside it; he had begun to imagine his future account to the extent of writing notes to himself that he then felt he had to destroy. It was thus increasingly near the end of the nine-month interval from the time of liberation, even as the train conveying him began to pass familiar cities and landmarks, nearing and then reaching Italy, that the compulsion to speak surfaced, intensified of course by the freedom to see and address an audience who would often be caught unawares, for whom the concentrationary world was often unknown or incredible—and frequently both.

Speaking, then, was the first recourse, requiring only the medium of a voice and encounters with people. Levi claimed an audience for this message among strangers he accosted during the journey as well as among the relatives and friends to whom he returned in the Turin community, whose responses to his accounts he found especially troubling: Auschwitz seemed to them, even as they listened sympathetically, a world too far from their own war experience, which had often involved suffering and hardship but was nonetheless, as Levi regarded it and even as atrocities can be at all compared, of a radically different order. Thus, also as a means of speaking in the absence of an immediate and live audience—and as a way of realizing a more stable form that might reach a broader group—Levi began writing. Impulsive as this basis for writing was, it was for Levi also a matter of principle: to record not only his own ordeal but the enormity of the Lager and the Nazi "project." It is not that Levi was not introspective: the authorial "I" did play a large role in his first book, written as it was constantly if not always in the first-person singular and in the genre of the memoir. But central even then were the acts and events themselves and his effort to analyze them: the why and how of their occurrence as he had experienced or witnessed them, most urgently, because they *had occurred.* The claim has been made, often critically, that Levi's focus was consistently on "personal" history, his own and that of other individuals, rather than on Holocaust history as such, but this confuses the material of his motivation with the historians' goal of a general understanding: for Levi, the general could be seen only through the particular. And Levi extended the distancing effect of this method also to his readers, whose reactions to the accounts were deliberately left to them, the events being shown but not, as narratives often do, dictating a response. Even when his narrative describes events that happened to himself, the significance of their retelling comes from the events and their causality, not because it was he who experienced and was recounting them.

As the narrative of the text—and its external history—unfold, however, it also becomes clear that there was more to the creation of *If This Is a Man* than Levi's description of its composition as spontaneous, innocent. For one thing, the backstory of Levi as a writer is more substantial than the impression he conveys. At least some of what he wrote as a student proved to be more than diversionary or casual jottings. So, for example, he would retain the 1943 poem "Crescenzago" (named for the Milan suburb where he was then working) among what would eventually become his published collected poems. Still more significant, he wrote versions in these prewar years of two of the "elements" ("Lead" and "Mercury") that later appeared in *The Periodic Table*—and, according to him, the foundation for the element of "Carbon" as well, the extraordinary conclusion of that book. Also during that time, Levi wrote a short story with the (prophetic?) title of "Uomo" (Man), which, although he refused to publish it when he undoubtedly could have done, he nonetheless retained among his records. Others of his efforts from the period have left few traces, but the samplings mentioned cast doubt on his claim that the first book lacked *any* literary intention. Even without the internal evidence that is also available, "literariness" would have been inescapable for the keen and retentive student that Levi had been. He himself acknowledged the continuing influence of one literature teacher in particular, Azelia Arici, from his liceo days; that his studies of literature at the school involved three languages in addition to Italian would also be salient.

Against a background of this sort, the question of whether Levi would have become a writer if not for the Auschwitz months becomes more complex than it might initially seem. Even if one views his wartime experience as a sufficient condition for his becoming a writer, this would not mean that without it he would not have followed the fork in the road which led to that destination. Levi himself at times agreed with this assessment, and not only because nobody could know what the outcome of any future contingencies would be, even in the extremity or the absence of Auschwitz. Certainly his studies and interests provided a basis for the later development, as they also cast doubt on his own claim of literary innocence after he did begin to write. But recognizing this does not contradict the urgency Levi reports as impelling the writing of *If This Is a Man: any* expression that is more than only phatic builds on forms and patterns spun out of much more than whole cloth for the occasion, no matter how original the work. Levi himself in the role of witness constantly attests that history is always present: even in the fraught setting of Auschwitz, Levi's schooldays memory restored for him passages from Dante on Ulysses, which he used then to teach Italian to his fellow Häftling, Pikolo. (Levi's account of these "lessons" appears in the section titled "The Canto of Ulysses.") Is it likely that nothing else from his liceo study of Dante remained with him?

There is, furthermore, substantial additional evidence, external and internal, that Levi's "autobiography" of his months in Auschwitz was meditated in both art and substance. So, for examples: the memoir first emerged in his hands as a manuscript of fourteen typed pages ("The Ten Last Days"). This then became the published book's concluding pages as Levi, working backward, filled the manuscript out with earlier episodes and reflections of the Lager months. Twelve years elapsed between the date attached to the first written entry of *If This Is a Man* (February 1946) and its eventual republication in 1958 by Einaudi of what stands now as the definitive version. The length of that interval itself would have made revisions of the text likely; between the time that the book's original completed version was first turned down in early 1947 by Einaudi and its eventual acceptance by another publisher later in the same year, he polished and revised. The principal editorial figure in the Einaudi rejection was Natalia Ginzburg, whose husband, Leone Ginzburg, had died under Nazi torture in 1944; a prominent literary figure in her own right, she subsequently found herself repeatedly explaining this negative decision on Levi's book, turning again and again to the phrase that it "was not the right time"—a common general reaction in the immediate post-Holocaust period, especially in Italy because of the early history of Italian fascism in relation to the Jewish community and then in Italy's wartime relation to Nazi Germany.

After one additional rejection (in another account, after *three* additional rejections; in any event, the turnaround time for these editorial and publishing decisions seems by current standards exceptionally short), the book was published in October 1947 by De Silva, a small press directed by Franco Antonicelli, which printed the book in a run of 2,500 copies. A substantial proportion of even that number remained unsold, and about a quarter of the total then warehoused in Florence was lost in the 1969 flood. Even before that, in 1952, Levi had returned to Einaudi to ask if they would reissue the book, but again the publisher's response was No. Finally, at the conclusion of still another round of discussions in 1955, Einaudi agreed to republish the book, but three more years would elapse before the new, final edition appeared. (Levi's initial difficulties in finding publishers for his writing in Italy characterized the history of his work's translations into other languages as well. The first translation into English of *If This Is a Man* appeared in

1959; the English translation of *The Periodic Table* appeared ten years after its Italian publication in 1975, having been rejected before that by more than twenty British publishers, and of *The Wrench*, nine years after its initial publication in 1978.)

How could this cumulative history of his first book, even if driven initially by impulse and urgency, *not* detract from Levi's claim of the spontaneous act of its composition? At the very least, his changes and additions to the text ensure that the book as it finally appeared was more deliberate and literary than the impulse that first motivated him. Those external considerations point to an artfulness that took Levi beyond history, and this is underscored by the text's own evidence—the way in which the text speaks *about* itself. Consider the opening and concluding sentences in the brief preface. Opening: "By my good fortune [*fortuna*], I was deported to Auschwitz only in 1944." And then in conclusion: "It seems to me superfluous to add that none of the facts [here] has been invented." But: "*Good fortune?*" *Auschwitz?* Levi quickly explains that he means by "good fortune" the shift in Nazi policy about survival in the camps, because by 1944 the prisoners' labor and thus their longer survival had come to seem, according to Levi, more valuable to the Germans than had been the case earlier. (This was not *universal* Nazi policy, as Levi suggests, but that is not the issue here.) Even with this quick explanation, however, the lead-in use of "good fortune" is startling and is clearly intended to be: an introduction to the voice that sustains a similar ironic distance in much of the narrative that follows. And indeed one "follows" quickly in the brief preface's concluding sentence. If it is "superfluous" to add that the "facts" cited in the book are indeed facts, why add that claim at all? Mentioning it increases little if anything of the text's credibility, but it speaks a good deal to the role of a figurative consciousness at work, the literary voice that the reader will be listening to in the text that follows. And of course it underscores the question that surfaces later in a variety of forms of what exactly Levi understands "facts" to be.

Not every reader, almost certainly including the author, will be fully conscious of the detailed artfulness of a written work. And although Levi's recollection of the urgency behind his writing might overshadow everything else in his memory, the process itself would unavoidably involve more than simply the impulse to write. Acknowledgment of a literary "unconscious" need not be unsettling even in a writer as self-conscious as Levi was; an "unconscious consciousness" seems to underlie all literary style—indeed, to be a ground for the phenomenon of style as such. However Flaubert struggled in searching for the mot juste, he made no decision to write *in the style* of Flaubert, a style that, before he created or found it, did not exist; like the individual brushstrokes of a painter, style appears also in the slightest detail of the written work—in syntax and grammar no less than in the broader flourishes of literary figuration—but not as a choice among alternatives that already exist. One could speak here of a "styleme" or atom of art: deliberate (in the sense of being neither accidental nor arbitrary) but also not meeting the standard requirements for making a choice, that is, for deciding between A or B with both those alternatives equally, actually present.

As Levi became a witness for other events, he appears here too as a witness, although in this case a witness against himself. At the most rudimentary level of evidence, there is the matter in *If This Is a Man* of the names of the personae who populate it. Ordinarily, the names of characters in an autobiography or memoir are assumed by readers to be their "actual" names: why wouldn't they be—unless, of course, the author informs the readers of specific substitutions and his reasons for making them. Romans à clef are not held accountable to historical criteria for the actions of characters who appear in them, but to imagine a memoir in which *all* the personae appear under fictional names would be a travesty—and Levi does not do that either. He does, however, change the names of certain of the characters he introduces. For one of the figures he describes— the dwarf Elias Lindzin—he makes the change specifically for the German translation of the book (to "David Kram"); for another, Lello Perugia, he uses *two* different names: Piero Sonnino in *If This Is a Man* (all editions) and Cesare in *The Truce*. Furthermore, he makes these changes without mentioning he is doing so; when in later references, he acknowledges having made them, it is almost always in response to objections to his descriptions by the individual characters themselves or by people close to them. (Whether those objections had a basis or not is a separate issue from questioning the use of fictional names themselves.)

Does this practice matter? Few readers would be troubled by or even interested in the difference between the names Levi assigns his characters and their actual names—since few would know any more about the characters than what Levi tells them; the names he assigns serve them as no more than markers or placeholders. Levi's later explanation of his use of pseudonyms as a matter of discretion or respect for privacy is credible, but it does not explain why he failed to mention the practice when he used it or why he used it for some figures but not others. In some instances where he did use actual names (as for "Sandro" [Delmastro]), furthermore, objections were later raised that might have been anticipated—underscoring how ad hoc Levi's decisions seem to have been. If Levi assumed that name changes in the text made no more difference than the names introduced in an openly fictional narrative, that reasoning would concede too much; it would certainly infringe on the concept of memoir or autobiography and on his professed adherence to "facts." So far as "discretion" was the motive, his efforts at disguise failed in virtually all their applications. Invariably, his representations of the personae in his autobiographies were close enough to reality to give the art away; thus, the autobiographies were ostensibly intended as factual—but *were* they?

That Levi minimizes the effect of artfulness in his first book might be explained by the compulsion he felt in writing it as leaving no space for indirection or sophistication, and perhaps this held also for what the book meant for him retrospectively once completed and published: testimony of the events and his life between his deportation to Auschwitz and his liberation. But it is clear that he *knew* as he wrote that he was altering details in the persons and events he described. Some of those changes may indeed have been inadvertent, but the evidence that he intended many, probably most, of them is as conclusive as such evidence can be—and he himself admitted this in retrospect: "It is possible that the distance in time [from the months in Auschwitz] has accentuated the tendency to round out the facts or heighten the color: this tendency, or temptation, is an integral part of writing. . . . Nevertheless, the episodes on which I have built each of these stories actually did take place." And elsewhere: "I've written two declaredly autobiographical books, with a large number of figures whom I tried to portray as they were, but I have no doubt that I reshaped them, even unconsciously."[3]

There are then, in the strict historical sense, misrepresentations in the autobiographies, and they appear often not as lapses of memory but as the result of deliberate reshaping of what and about whom he is writing. That "Henri" (Paul Steinberg) is in Levi's account twenty-eight years old instead of his actual seventeen and, against counterevidence, homosexual may seem no weightier than the alteration of his name. Also in other later autobiographical accounts—for example, Levi's references to his athletic achievements as a student running the 800-meter race—the star athlete of his class, "Guido," whom he mentions in those accounts, has described Levi's account of his own accomplishments as imaginary: "Levi tried hard,"

according to the actual "Guido," "but he never came close."[4]
Then, too, Levi's description in *The Periodic Table* of Guido's
quasi-athletic feat of having stripped naked during a class when
the teacher's back was turned and dressing himself again before
the teacher turned around simply never happened, according
to Guido. The tagline currently used, apparently as reassur-
ance, for certain literary or cinematic works as "based on a true
story" would be excessive if attached to Levi's memoirs, but it is
literally accurate for parts of those writings, with Levi himself
aware of the fact. Still a question remains, even if this contention were granted, what difference it makes for characterizing
Levi's writings as history or even as memoir, thus also in terms
of placing them in relation to literary genre and to both their
literary and extraliterary force. These questions are the more
pressing because of Levi's repeated claims for the influence
of science and its methods on his writing: the combination of
rigor and economy that he found essential in the former and
again in the latter. In addressing this issue, the narrower question emerges of what Levi's broadest ideals for writing *were* and
how he judged other writers in relation to those ideals: this as
a further step to understanding how close Levi himself came to
realizing them.

LEVI ON WRITERS AND WRITING

Several converging lines bear on this topic, one of which
is especially useful for inferring Levi's own ideals or principles
of writing: what he has to say about *other* writers, as he speaks
of them positively or, at times, critically. Despite his custom-
ary understatement, he provides enough information outlining
virtues and faults in the writings of these others to provide an
outline also of his own credo. His most telling comments along
these lines appear in the unusual anthology of selections from
works that were significant for him when he encountered them

and/or for their continuing influence on his own writing—his attempt, as he puts it in the preface to the volume (*The Search for Roots: A Personal Anthology*, 1981)—to "bring to light the possible traces of what has been read on what has been written . . . a bloodless experiment."[5] A gross anatomy, in other words, that would reveal from his external history the internal genealogy and aims of his writing.

This volume itself was projected as part of an Einaudi series of similar collections by distinguished authors. In the event, Levi's was the only volume published in the series, although its value for understanding Levi as writer—and person—is unaffected by that. He himself would later say that in making his selections for the book, "I felt more exposed to the public, more unbosomed . . . than in writing my own books; . . . I felt more exposed . . . than in any of my first-person writings"—a striking confession by a writer widely known for the scrupulousness of his first-person autobiographies.[6] The book, then, provides at least as intimate a view of Levi's interests and literary ideals as any other of his works, certainly as much as any of his assessments of other writers, including those who either exceeded or failed to meet the criteria he applied in shaping the selections—and were thus omitted from the volume.

The selections excerpted in the anthology are notably diverse. Among them are pages from a chemistry textbook that Levi first encountered as a university student: *Laboratory Methods of Organic Chemistry* by Ludwig Gattermann; he includes a section from that text titled "On the Prevention of Accidents," which Levi reports he had consulted "hundreds of times" and virtually memorized. He also includes selections from Thomas Mann's *Joseph and His Brothers*, as well as entries by Rabelais and Sholem Aleichem, Joseph Conrad and Isaac Babel. There, too, appear "Why Are Animals Beautiful?" from Darwin's *Origin of Species* and a selection from Lucretius's *On the Nature of Things*. The reader encounters Lucretius shortly after a selection from Melville's *Moby-Dick;* Bertrand Russell's answer to "Why We Are Not Happy" appears soon after a selection from the book of Job with which Levi begins the anthology. Homer, Jonathan Swift, T. S. Eliot, Saint-Exupéry, Giuseppe Belli, Marco Polo, and Paul Celan are also represented, together with several contemporary Italian writers who were less well-known internationally (Mario Rigoni Stern, Stefano D'Arrigo) and the French author Roger Vercel whose sea novel *Tugboat* was given to Levi as a parting gift in the Auschwitz infirmary when the camp was being abandoned by the Germans *and,* in Levi's own words "on a day (18 January 1945) when I expected to die."[7] It was the first book that Levi, a constant reader since his schooldays, had held in his hands in more than a year. (Levi writes in his prefatory note to this selection that he knew nothing about the author, either at first reading or thirty-five years later when he composed the anthology: an odd indifference for so resourceful a seeker.)

What conclusions follow from this unusual assortment? Levi emphasizes that in the volume he is looking at himself as if he were an external observer. About two of the selections he notes that he is retrieving a text and an author that marked a place in his life rather than because of their influence on his writing or thought (these references are to *Tugboat* and Saint-Exupéry's *Wind, Sand, and Stars*). Even with all the diversity, however, certain common themes on the art and craft of writing emerge: the importance Levi attaches to clarity, precision, and method, all of which are assumed as necessary in scientific texts or discourse but which he registers here as a standard for *all* texts or discourse. To be sure, these are not unfamiliar as literary values either, but they appear less conventional when represented in the volume by excerpts from the transgressive and exuberant work of writers like Rabelais and Swift. But for Levi, any apparent inconsistency by his inclusion of the latter is outweighed by his insistence that for them as for the others, *they* accept the limits and consistency from which satire and irony and not least of all transgression set out. Levi expresses that same impulse in advocating the literary representations of characters who find themselves severely tested by formidable challenges—challenges from nature, from other people, most of all from themselves. These he finds in Melville, Conrad, Babel—and there can be no doubt of this presence, albeit more ominous, in his own writings about the Holocaust. (Jack London, a longtime favorite of Levi's for having enlarged on these themes, is an unexplained absence here.)

Levi wrote often about his own favorite and life-long hobby of mountain climbing in terms exemplifying these same challenges; it seems fair to infer that the act of writing—in authors who turned explicitly to such themes but also in those who did not—represented a response to a challenging world of experience that invited, at times demanded, a perilous reshaping or remaking. Writing in this respect echoed for him the classical Greek tradition in which literature was an instance of poesis, a "making" in the sense of a craft, skill, or technique. In other words, a literary "theme" in even the most imaginative literary works is for Levi more than a subject to be worked at or over; the combination of daring and discipline required for enlarging on the subjects becomes also a feature of the writing as writing, recognizable even when art itself attempts to conceal its art, as it so often and skillfully does. Under this pressure, form and content are for Levi closely bound to each other, aspects of a single literary "self."

Notable omissions other than London figure elsewhere in the volume. Some of these Levi explains as due not to literary failings but to the contrary: "I have deliberately excluded names that are (or should be) part of the patrimony of all, such as Dante, Leopardi, Manzoni, Flaubert, etc.: to have included them would be like writing on an ID card as identifying marks, 'two eyes.'" But then too, certain omissions are for cause. So

Levi mentions the absence of Dostoyevsky and Balzac as likely candidates whom he has forced himself to read only "out of duty, late, wearily, and with little profit"—adding elsewhere that Dostoyevsky would have been a better writer had he reduced what he wrote by a third. And of Balzac's extended oeuvre he says summarily: "Life is too short." Kafka does not appear in this anthology of writers to whom Levi felt close; he was never, Levi says guardedly, "one of my favorite authors"—admitting this although (arguably *because*) he had himself translated *The Trial* into Italian for an Einaudi series. It is Kafka's view of life that puts him off, Levi notes, the darkness that seemed to become progressively stronger: "He fears punishment, and at the same time desires it . . . a sickness within Kafka himself"—a contradiction for which Levi's optimism and commitment to reason could find no place, however he recognized their *possible* coexistence. (Levi writes elsewhere quite flatly that he does not believe Max Brod's report that Kafka could not stop laughing when reading aloud to members of his Prague circle some newly written pages of *The Trial*.) He includes Paul Celan's "Death Fugue" in the anthology but remains nonetheless severely critical of Celan's poetry more generally: "What can you say if the [poet's] message is coded and no one has the key?" Elsewhere he goes so far as to speak about Celan and Georg Trakl as "the two least decipherable poets writing in German," extending this comment even to suggest a causal link between their suicides and the opacity of their poetry. Presumably the hyperbole here is not intended as a general rule, but it further emphasizes the importance for Levi of clarity and intelligibility in writing as moral and not only aesthetic qualities: "I can't stand writers like Beckett; it is the duty of every human being to communicate. The same goes for the likes of Ezra Pound: writing in Chinese simply showed a disrespect for the reader. Writing should be a public service." And about Borges, too, admitting that he had not read very much of his work (itself a tell-tale on the part of a voracious reader): "I would say I have a veiled dislike for him. I see something in Borges that is alien and distant from me"—leaving unsaid what the "something" is, although for readers of Levi and Borges, not much of a mystery: Borges was a writer who was willing to leave the reader dangling in midair—something that Levi would not do unless the author were also left dangling alongside. With Proust, the problem is not silence or lack of clarity or irony at its extreme but something akin to their opposites: he is, more simply, "boring."[8]

The criteria underlying these judgments are more than pieties for Levi, although they are not intended to be interpreted narrowly. This is evident in the often complex and understated sentences of his own writing that assume the reader's collaboration in much more than the elementary act of knowing a language. He is well aware, as his comment on Proust indicates, that if clarity is a necessary condition of good writing, it is not sufficient, since an author, as an alternative to being clear and boring, can also be "clear and useless, clear and untruthful, clear and vulgar." And then, too, these hybrid forms of clarity are not the only potential literary faults. Wordiness or excess in quantity or emotive quality also count against writers. If Dostoyevsky would have benefitted by cutting his writings by a third, Levi intimates a similar criticism of Isaac Bashevis Singer, about whom his restrained public comments differ markedly from his private ones. When Singer won the Nobel Prize in 1978, Levi praised him in *La Stampa* for his "rare honesty," at the same time writing in a letter to a friend at Einaudi, "I don't like Singer at all." And later: "He writes too much, and so he seems too thin." And about Elie Wiesel's work, Levi is notably evasive. Aware that Wiesel's writings on the subject of the Holocaust were, at least initially, much more widely known than his, it is clear from what Levi both does and does not say that he felt strongly about what he saw as a substantial *liter-*

ary difference between himself and Wiesel. Thus, to an interviewer's provocative question directed at a comparison, "What do you think of Elie Wiesel?" Levi responded so guardedly that one has to look twice to see the point: "Elie Wiesel chose a different path from mine, but in my opinion his personal history justified him. . . . I do not find any artifice in his keeping faith." A literary judgment by way of evasion.[9]

Writers often seem to judge writers contemporary with themselves (thus also competitors) by replacing the adage "About the dead one should speak only good" with "One should speak good *only* about the dead": living authors are collectively viewed as fair game. Levi, to the contrary, was ready to praise some of the living and to criticize also some of the dead who had won honored places. So he speaks often and admiringly about such contemporary authors as Umberto Saba, Italo Calvino, Natalia Ginzburg (notwithstanding her editorial role in rejecting *If This Is a Man*), Saul Bellow, even—this perhaps surprisingly—Philip Roth, whom he read late in life. When he does comment negatively about living authors, he is almost always responding to a direct question about the specific author.

Even so, many of his assessments of other authors may seem unusually sharp, and it is relevant for understanding this intensity to reiterate the importance for Levi of values embodied in writing that are not exclusively literary: his commitment to writing as closely bound to moral and political ideals in which issues of right and wrong, justice and injustice are intrinsic. The claim of such connections is not original; an established tradition in literary and stylistic theory had emphasized it, encapsulated in Buffon's brief statement that "style is the man himself." The part of the twentieth century which imprinted itself so decisively on Levi provided as much evidence for this view as any other period in history, since the political values of fascism and totalitarianism—force, imperative, repetition, hyperbole—imposed themselves on *all* the expressive forms: on writing and rhetoric as markedly as on architecture, painting, or music.

What is distinctive in Levi's emphasis on this relation is his view of it through the lens of scientific method, which is for him not beyond values but expressive of his constant quarrel with evasion, unclarity, tendentiousness. The scientific ideal of challenging those qualities on moral and formal grounds has itself often been criticized as advocating science's own illusory version of the Garden of Eden, extolling an impossible dream, a wistful view from nowhere. To whatever extent this criticism of objectivity applies to Levi's position, that ideal nonetheless comes closer in his view to avoiding the faults of mystification or obscurantism—or authoritarianism—than any of the alternatives historically proposed to it. If his judgments of other authors or individual works seem at times exaggerated, his criticism consistently applies the values he finds intrinsic to writing itself. In displaying this commitment, that stance further undercuts the objection often directed at Levi of a fundamental moral and stylistic reserve or distance: Levi as nonjudgmental, detached. This is surely as fundamental a misreading as has been directed at any major literary figure. The fact of such commitment is obviously not itself a warrant for Levi's individual judgments; his criticism of Samuel Beckett, for example, seems especially problematic given Levi's own reliance on literary silence and irony. But again, the purpose of reviewing his comments on other authors is not to defend his judgments of them but to infer the criteria he applied in making them—criteria that presumably he would accept also as standards or guides for his own writing.

From Levi's assessment of other writers in these ways, what might be called a unified field theory of writing emerges that seems meant to apply across languages, genres, disciplines, or modes of expression: a theory of discourse. The claims of clarity, plain speaking, accessibility—along with economy, conciseness—which thus appear as primary for all communication have heightened importance in literature, as their opposites also represent larger faults in what is, after all, language epitomized. These qualities of writing are not merely matters of technique; they rest on moral grounds in the way that communication as a whole does. Writing for Levi is a moral act, much as William Strunk, Jr., and E. B. White claim in their *Elements of Style:* "The approach to style is by way of plainness, simplicity, orderliness, sincerity. . . . Muddiness is not merely a disturber of prose; it is also a destroyer of life, of hope." Levi is not saying, as Strunk and White in their handbook suggest, that since complexity and difficulty are in principle always reducible or available for simplification, they *should* be reduced. Levi himself wrote about difficult subjects—difficult conceptually as well as emotionally. He often made severe demands of his readers, requiring them at once to distinguish and then to relate the various layers of his writing (a conception of his work as he himself described it). But where such difficulty or complexity occurs, it must be earned, warranted by the difficulty of the subject matter itself. Thus Levi had no hesitation in turning to chemical formulas or equations where the findings he was exploring depended on them—and as he attempted to lead the reader through them, again always insofar as the subject written about required their introduction. *And* as they answered on the other side to a common principle of economy: nothing more in the representation than the subject required.

THEORY IN PRACTICE: THE POETRY, TRANSLATIONS, NOVELS

Poetry was for Levi a constant resource to which he turned with greater emphasis at some times than others but which remained for him a ready and continuing means of literary expression from his student days on. So, for example, in 1946, at the same time he was shaping *If This Is a Man,* he wrote four-teen of the slightly more than sixty poems that he would even-tually publish. Two volumes of poetry appeared in his lifetime: *L'osteria di Brema* (1975) and *Ad ora incerta* (1984; published in English as *Shema: Collected Poems* and *Collected Poems,* respec-tively, both translated by Ruth Feldman and Brian Swann)—the latter including all the poems of the first volume and additional ones. The posthumous edition of his *Collected Poems* that ap-peared in 1992 included all the poems published earlier as well as some that had remained unpublished. That Levi's poetry was taken up by only a small readership reflected poetry's relatively small readership generally; it also reflected the specific interests of many of Levi's readers, who had come to his work through his two earliest books. But it also bears at some level on his po-etry itself and Levi's resistance there to following poetic fash-ion or to going beyond what a number of the few critics who reviewed his books of poetry found to be its sententious and literalist style. To be sure, those charges might be warranted without detracting from the poetry's other values, but they do not add to them, and it seems clear that taken on its own terms, Levi's poetry would not have made even the mark it did except through the impact of his other writing. If one compares his poems to those of similar scope by poets like W. B. Yeats or Wallace Stevens—both of an older generation, but overlapping with Levi chronologically—the difference in inventiveness and imaginative range is evident. It is the literal that is preponder-ant in his work, detracting from the individual work as from the genre.

In part because of this same emphasis, however, the poems are proportionately revealing of Levi the person. Many of them are written in direct address to "you" (singular or plu-ral), a conventional form of lyric poetry that allows the author greater freedom to speak in his own first-person voice. So, for example, Levi's poem to Lucia on her sixtieth birthday, with the date as its title: "12 July 1980." The poem opens with the line "Have patience, my weary lady"—and concludes, perhaps with greater restraint than its recipient might have hoped for, with: "Accept to please me, these fourteen lines./They are my rough way of saying how dear you are,/And that I wouldn't be in this world without you." Among this group are the two poems that allude in veiled terms to Levi's fellow partisans whom the partisans themselves executed: "Epitaph" (1952), addressed to "you who pass by this hill," and "Partisan" (1981), addressed to all the partisans, living and dead. And it includes the poem with the striking title "For Adolf Eichmann" (1960), addressing Eichmann and wishing him instead of the death he *would* suffer that he might "live longer than anyone ever lived./ . . . sleepless five million nights,/And may you be visited each night by the suffering of everyone who saw."[10]

Levi's published translations into Italian have understandably attracted comparatively slight attention, but certain of their features bear directly on his conception of writing. As mentioned, he translated for publication six books from English, French, German, and (ostensibly) Dutch—with a good knowledge of the first three languages added to his acute literary sensibility, though even then not meeting the standards ordinarily expected of a professional translator. For one of the books, his translation of Mary Douglas's *Natural Symbols* (1979), his handling of its content as well as of the language drew criticism. His 1983 translation of Kafka's *Der Prozess* (The Trial) brought both praise and criticism. That project bears directly on his conception of writing in part because it was Kafka whom he was translating but still more because of his later discussion of certain decisions he made in doing the translation. So, for example: "I diverged at times [from the original]. Confronted with certain harsh, rough moments, I pared them down, I cut up some of the sentences. I had no hesitation in this, as long as the meaning remained. Kafka has no compunction in using repetition, in the course of ten lines he repeats the same word three or four times. I tried to avoid this."[11]

This is a notably daring statement in relation to an author of Kafka's stature, still more so about a writer as austere as Kafka. However one might defend Levi's decisions here or the theory of translation they presuppose, he introduces them without elaboration and as if unaware of how contentious they are. The liberties endorsed in these statements are the more striking because of the close and literalist scrutiny Levi gave the translations of his own work, especially the English and the German translations of *If This Is a Man*, for which he insisted on virtually full collaboration. The translations from the French of Claude Lévi-Strauss's *La voie des masques* (The Way of the Masks) and *Le regard éloigné* (The View from Afar) in 1984 and 1985, respectively, were well received, as was the translation of Jacques Presser's *De Nacht der Girondijnen* (*The Night of the Girondists*), which Levi had translated in 1976 from the original Dutch (he evidently came to Dutch through his knowledge of German; there is no other evidence of his having studied or spoken the language). In relation to his study of Yiddish when he was writing *If Not Now, When?* he claimed to have translated Moshe Kaganovic's *Die Milkhomeh fun di Jiddische Partisaner in Mizrach-Europa* (The War of the Jewish Partisans in Eastern Europe), but there is no record of how much of that translation was completed or whether it was ever published.

With the exception of his translation of the Presser book that Levi initiated because of his high regard for it, his motivation for undertaking the work of these translations was largely economic; especially after his retirement from SIVA, Levi often expressed concern about finances. (He undertook the Kafka translation as part of the Einaudi series Writers Translated by Writers.) But that motive by itself would not explain why Levi, typically modest in claims about himself, felt qualified to undertake translations from languages over which he had less than the full command ordinarily expected for published translation. Literary internationalism did have a head start over its political and economic counterparts in Europe, but another explanation suggests itself as still likelier—drawn from Levi the chemist and intimated in the statement of his purpose in the Kafka translation to articulate "*the* meaning" of the text (emphasis added). Implicit in the definite article he includes here is an ideal of language as universally translatable because of a core meaning that transcends other differences among the languages, such as their grammar, idioms, or emphases, which then become historical accidents and in this sense extralinguistic. (That the Inuit would have more words for types of snow than people in places who saw less of it, as Benjamin Lee Whorf had pointed out, says nothing about the translatability of one language into another.)

A ready model of this view of translation for Levi would have been the language of science, with its fundamental requirement that all claims or reasoning be stated in such a form that they—the claims and their referents—can be duplicated or found in any other cultural or linguistic setting. On this account, not only natural languages but individual or group forms of expression, including those involving local conventions of literary genre and figurative discourse, become subordinate to core meaning; an approximation of this belief is implied in Levi's account of the changes in his Kafka translation as nonetheless preserving "the [text's] meaning." Only so, it seems, would the units of discourse in one language be translatable into those of another language—in effect, as atoms of meaning. It is not that Levi did not take the act of translation seriously; in an essay on translation, he writes that "the translator is the only one who truly reads a text." But again, how a translator would read particular texts would be limited (or in Levi's thinking, enhanced) by the definition of *meaning* he invokes here.

Levi writes most fully about the implications of these and

his other ideals of writing in his 1978 novel *The Monkey's Wrench* (in its British title, *The Wrench*). Here Levi follows the adventures of Faussone, a rigger hired to solve structural and mechanical problems around the globe, who in that work finds himself often in challenging, even dangerous situations. In the novel, Faussone recounts a series of episodes to a narrator who happens to be a chemist and author; the narrator is freed in the text by Faussone's accounts of *his* craft to speak about his own. The chemist-author-narrator cannot simply be assumed to be Levi himself, but the correspondence is difficult to ignore. So, for example, the chemist-author-narrator reflects on how much writers and riggers have in common: There is "the advantage of being able to test yourself . . . the pleasure of seeing your work grow, beam after beam, bolt after bolt, solid, necessary, symmetrical, suited to its purpose; and when it's finished you look at it and you think that it will be of use to someone you don't know." The analogy proposed here between writing and the crafts is sustained, although the narrator finds in writing a measure of freedom and with it a measure of irresponsibility that the rigger cannot afford: "One of the writer's great privileges is the possibility of remaining imprecise and vague, saying and not saying, inventing freely, beyond any rule of caution. After all, on the towers we construct they don't run any high-tension lines; if our structures fall, nobody gets killed. In other words, we're irresponsible, and no writer has ever been put on trial or sent to jail because his constructions came apart." Failures, of course, are not only possible but common to both—and the narrator reminds Faussone that the writer himself may find that what he has written is "a botch, silly, incomplete, excessive, futile." The starting point of the analogy between rigging and writing is significant, not only because Levi sees them both as involving "jobs of work"—chores—but also skills, procedures demanding to be applied as they should be. Both the rigger's and the writer's work are crafts involving technique and precision, with the consequences of failure and the pleasure of accomplishment quickly evident in both. (The novel itself drew criticism from the political left in Italy because of its praise of job labor, which would include, as Levi argued in his own defense against the criticism, factory labor.)[12]

The model of a scientific experiment is never far off here; the title of the excerpt from Gattermann's chemistry text, "On the Prevention of Accidents," in *The Search for Roots* might well serve as the title of the primer on writing or style that Levi himself never wrote. Economy is also part of the ideal: "Maximum information with minimum clutter." And then, too, whatever else clarity entails, it does not mean superficiality or even ease of access. "A clear text is not perforce elementary; it can be read at several levels"—itself a warning about the potential misunderstanding of his list of ideal qualities.[13] George Orwell, when he writes in his essay "Politics and the English Language" that "good prose is like a window pane," does not deny that the subjects of writing viewed through the "window pane" may vary in complexity and difficulty, but he offers no hints on how writing about complex subjects would be able to manage that difference without fault. By contrast, Levi, beginning with the etymology of the names of the chemical elements and then going on to the extended chemical formulas and procedures of laboratory analysis, recognized the technical difficulty of much scientific discourse for readers with no foundation to build on, and he wrote about this; he was willing at times to compel the reader—assuming that reader wished to continue reading—to learn on the spot technical details of the subject, for which Levi himself would serve as instructor. The implication of such accounts would then be that clarity requires only *as much* clarity as the subject permits, with the corollary that even the clearest of texts may nonetheless pose difficulties for understanding or explication. These formal conditions for writing join with certain practical ones (in a particularly gentle example, Levi recommends a "rest period in a drawer" between the first and final drafts of a manuscript), but these too are subordinate to a much larger and more fundamental condition that Levi saves for last: "O, I forgot to tell you, that in order to write, one must have something to write."[14]

Many of Levi's readers, including some of his strongest admirers and advocates, regard as his least successful—more openly, his *unsuccessful*—full-length work the novel, *If Not Now, When?* (1984). This judgment clashes with what had been the novel's popular success in Italy, but however one understands that contrast, the critically adverse comments made about the book advance the important and largely neglected question of where to place Levi in the landscape of literary history. To do this poses more difficulties in relation to Levi than to many authors, and not only or even primarily because of the variety of genres in which he wrote. By standard literary conventions, *If Not Now, When?* is a novel, and what Levi has to say as he himself emphasizes its place in that genre and in his explanation of that emphasis offers a valuable perspective on his oeuvre as a whole. Partly in response to some of the criticism directed against the book, Levi's comments about it address issues of literary theory more fully than for any other of his writings. So, for example, he reports that in this book he experienced for the first time the true freedom of the novelist: the space in which to create characters in effect ex nihilo, to give them identities and lines of development and decision without being bound by historical or any other presumptive constraints. The implication here is that by contrast all his previous writing *had been* bound to its subjects by the intractability of those constraints, which one assumes to be their historical, scientific, and personal underpinning. Admittedly, Levi notes that even in *If Not Now, When?* characters and events that began life entirely as his creations soon declared their independence, becoming increasingly self-determinate, forging their own way and making their own choices. Even as this occurred, however, it was not an external historical or factual template that set the course of those developments but physical and psychological causality, which would be unavoidable in any account of human agency.

In point of fact, however, the author's freedom that Levi celebrates in recounting the novel's origins was not, and could not have been, as radical as he described it. Insofar as the category "Holocaust novels" applies to any writings about the Holocaust, *If Not Now, When?* must surely be among them, with the category itself circumscribing the events and characters that appear in it. And it is quickly evident in the novel that not only Levi's own partisan experience affects the narrative but also the extensive historical research he undertook as background for the novel: his reading about the groups of Jewish partisans in eastern Europe, his study of the Yiddish-speaking communities of eastern Europe more generally and, by his own account, his study of Yiddish itself. (It is unclear how far that study took him, but his knowledge of German would have been an important aid; his eye for linguistic nuance was in any event sufficiently sharpened to bring him to the epigraph for *The Periodic Table:* "Ibergekumene tsores iz gut tsu dertseylin" [Troubles overcome are good to recount].)

Still, there was no basic template on which Levi patterned the novel, as there had been in *The Monkey's Wrench*, where Faussone's character, work, and adventures answered to accounts that Levi had heard elsewhere and even briefly observed himself aboard a pipe-laying ship off Sicily. And of course it would also be different in this respect from Levi's "autobiographical" writings, even when they at times deviated from the actual events or characters presented in them. Those of his short stories sometimes characterized as "science fiction" are, as the genre science fiction necessarily does, reacting against "science *non*-fiction," about which of course Levi knew a great deal. Levi's two autobiographies as well as *The Periodic Table* and his last book, *The Drowned and the Saved*, are certainly not fiction in that category's usual connotation or in Levi's own understanding of it. Quite aside from the issue of their historical accuracy, those other works differ structurally from *If Not Now, When?* insofar as they draw on an integral but also implicit historical template or base; the contrast between this and the authorial freedom about which Levi enthuses in referring to *If Not Now, When?* is notable both for his unusual enthusiasm and for his explanation of it.

On the other hand, a distinctive and also, in Levi's writings, unusual feature of *If Not Now, When?* is the prominence of conventional historical conclusions and generalizations about the "Final Solution" as it was implemented in eastern Europe. He introduces this historical background and framework, furthermore, in conjunction with the "free," self-motivated activities of the novel's characters, and here it is as if Levi, without the grist of specific personal occurrences or events that bring life to his other writings, seems forced to summon historical generalizations to fill the gap. But the turn to such abstractions (however accurately reported and formulated), especially in a work designed as a novel, instead makes the novel itself thinner and more mechanical, straining the narrative development in ways quite different from the less explicit generalizations that Levi brings to life by way of character and action in his other writings. It is always risky to speak of a writer's "natural" medium, but there is also reason, certainly temptation for doing so. We cannot know how Homer would have fared (or did fare) as a lyric poet or dramatist, but one might reasonably predict different levels of achievement as he worked among those genres—as one finds more immediately in the contrasting distance between Goethe's poetry and his prose. A similar difference seems to apply to Levi in the contrast between this novel and his other writings. One way of understanding the awkwardness of *If Not Now, When?* is through Levi's difficulty with the very freedom he celebrates as its basis, the contrast between what he experienced as his liberation from "fact" in its writing and his other, more fully realized works, which, viewed externally, were openly grounded in history and its facts without succumbing to them. In other words, by putting history in its literary place.[15]

The criticism cited here is similar to that leveled in relation to Levi's poetry: its sententiousness, its literalness, its impeded imaginative grasp. In the case of the poetry, the problem was Levi's writing within his favored limits in a genre that called for more—and this same limitation seems to apply also to *If Not Now, When?* It is as if the freedom opened for him in those two genres as he conceived of them was too broad and boundless to provide Levi's imaginative power with the purchase on which he had otherwise relied: the absent grain of sand that provided the imaginative friction—and then pearl—of his writing as it moved easily and naturally between the particular and the general. Levi himself wrote explicitly about the difference between being a "novelist" and the role he understood for himself as author of his autobiographical writings: "Writing about things seen is easier than invention. . . . It is describing: you have a trail, you dig into your close or distant memories, put the specimens in order . . . then you pick up a trail of mental causes and snap. . . . In every case you are guided, held by the hand by the facts."[16] In these, his own terms, it is not Levi the "novelist" for whom writing comes more easily and freely but Levi in his more typical role as narrator, whether in his memoirs or in his reflective essays like those in *The Drowned and the Saved* or in his forays into scientific curiosities in his science fiction.

LEVI'S LITERARY PLACE

How closely does Levi's own work realize the ideals he professes in judging other writers? Again, the criteria of precision, economy, and clarity remain as necessary but not sufficient conditions; few readers of Levi would fault him for failing to meet them in most of his writings. But those qualities are present only in some and arguably not the most compelling of his work, where an unusual combination of imaginative range and moral evocation motivates writing that is at times meant to be historical and not imagined, at other times meant to display the intricacies of the natural order (also, after all, historical) as itself having moral force. Levi himself acknowledged that nothing he had written about the Lager added much—arguably anything—to the cumulative accounts assembled by professional historians about either the death camps or the more numerous concentration and labor camps. But he shows clearly how a grasp of historical "data" may bring out angles, implications, understructure about which the data themselves typically— necessarily; it's not the fault of the data—remain mute: it is the imagination proving that it has the capacity for envisioning and displaying the data in ways that the data themselves do not and cannot envision and display themselves. Kant's supporting statement for his Copernican revolution, that "concepts without intuitions are empty, intuitions without concepts are blind," has few more vivid exemplifications than the way in which Levi brings into view the conjunction of historical particulars with moral concepts.

The role of the imagination has been typically associated with art and the aesthetic, but this is an arbitrarily narrow understanding of the concept. Levi demonstrates this from a number of directions without making an issue of the demonstration. So, for example, in order to see how the *moral* imagination can reveal distinctive aspects of nature's intricacies and turns, one has only to grasp the startling features of nature, human and nonhuman, that Levi puts on display, with a moral sensibility there clearly directing the imagination. When he notices, for example, the crucial role that containers play in nature—citing examples from eggshells to furs to the shape of the human body—it becomes quickly evident how much more than only a conceptual abstraction the idea and role of nature are for him. (The human skin he refers to here includes his own: "I know more beautiful, more sturdy, and more picturesque skins; but it would seem to me unnatural to exchange them for mine.")[17] It may not seem that being able to determine whether an egg is hard-boiled by looking at it without breaking the shell is morally relevant, any more than is the question of how fleas can jump more than a hundred times their length when the best-trained human athletes are limited to jumping only five times theirs. But the impulse of inquiry and understanding behind these investigations becomes unintelligible unless one registers a moral thread in their source, a means of at once distinguishing and identifying the human— and one that is more than only utilitarian. Those and other such improbable findings, Levi shows, are significant humanly, not simply and extraneously for eggs or fleas.

The enormity of the Shoah as an event adds its historical and moral weight to Levi's writing when he turns to it explicitly and as it shadows much else in his writing. But one need only recall how banal and exploitative writings about the Holocaust have often been to recognize also the achievement of writing about that event without imposing on it ideological prescriptions or the writer's own claims of presence and self. Levi's writing about the Holocaust has at times been faulted as being *too* distant or remote from the event and its victims— disinterested (not uninterested) to a fault. That claim is open to discussion, but a common absence in its several versions is a failure to recognize the effort, indeed the passion, required of someone who had undergone Levi's experience to write about it in the dispassionate voice of Levi's narrators. As it required a masterful author to evoke in an audience the impulse to shout out and warn Othello of Iago's treachery in order to prevent

Desdemona's murder and at the same time to keep the audience silent and in their seats—a distancing that at once intensifies and contains their reaction (Kant's "purposiveness without purpose" in the *Critique of Judgment*)—so Levi writes about history as he does about nature, from the basic conviction of the link between them: factual even as qualified by the human perspective on them. Levi recognizes the dangers of "aestheticizing" history, especially human history. The distancing effect in Levi's writing has at times been mistaken for a refusal to pass moral judgment, a charge of aestheticization. But moral no less than aesthetic judgment is a constant presence in Levi's writing, often subtle and implied—in this sense, distant—but even more forceful because of the understatement, the rejection of hyperbole.

There would undoubtedly be disagreement among Levi's readers if they were asked to rank his best or most original or most compelling writings, and it would be difficult to achieve a consensus on what criteria to apply even in attempting such judgment. There would be much less dispute, however, about which among Levi's writings were distinctively his—that is, that would have been unlikely, certainly *less* likely, to have been written by anyone else. Even if that standard may not be very informative, it seems relatively uncontroversial that *The Periodic Table* would stand foremost in this respect. Other writers, including some with greater standing than Levi as scientists, have brought scientific analysis and narrative to life, with Darwin a ready example here. But the imaginative structure that finds the table of physical elements informative about the reach of personal history has few if any predecessors or competitors in the literary or scientific or historical worlds. *The Periodic Table* is clearly a literary work, not one primarily of either science or history: literary not only in the sense that the narrative voice has a significant presence in the exposition (as it often does even in writing that purports to block it, a common feature of standard scientific writing) but that the voice is also a subject of the writing. This is a common feature of the memoir as a genre, but it would be difficult to mistake *The Periodic Table* for a memoir; the inventiveness of the narrator's voice reveals it not as "remembered" but as a feature of the literary present.[18]

It is difficult to find precedents or competitors for a work in which science and history, used as grist for a personal literary narrative, yield *The Periodic Table*'s combination of adventure and moral instruction. It is not only that few readers or authors would even think of the *possibilities* inherent in the qualities of elements: that "Distilling is beautiful" ("Potassium") or that zinc is a "boring" element—or that argon, one of the inert, noble, and rare gases, bears a striking resemblance through those qualities to Levi's Piedmont Jewish ancestors. But readers also learn more about those ancestors to support the claim of resemblance, with some striking asides about the individual ancestors and others about the Hebrew inlay in the Piedmontese dialect that produces such charms, among the clothing merchants, as *na vesta a kinim* for a polka-dot dress: *kinim* being a reference to the lice memorably known as one of the Ten Plagues inflicted on the Egyptians to pressure Pharaoh to permit the Exodus. The constant moral presence in Levi's writing does not rely on implication, since Levi speaks of it explicitly, in broad as well as limited strokes. He writes in "Potassium," for example, about the periodic table, chemistry more generally, and his reasons for placing himself close to them: "Chemistry led to the heart of Matter, and Matter was our ally precisely because the Spirit, dear to Fascism, was our enemy." The background to such a claim, like its justification, was taken for granted by Levi. Fascism had looked to the tradition of philosophical Idealism for its rationale, to thinkers like Giovanni Gentile and the early Benedetto Croce for whom "mere" science and its assumed materialism were subordinate to the reach of the ideal or spirit that, in their view, was not only prior but a source and in effect a lawgiver. The horrific consequences of its actions make it easy to forget that fascism had looked to philosophical Idealism as its conceptual forebear: not only to nonmaterialism, but to *antimaterialism*, an applied form of practical and conceptual reasoning that provoked Levi's lifelong opposition.

All of which brings the discussion back to Levi as writer, the qualities that give his work their combination of breadth, intensity, and interest. Here the significance begins to become clearer of an issue that has remained largely absent from the substantial secondary literature about Levi and his writing— neglected in work where, more typically, all possible and many improbable questions are asked: a literary version of the mystery of Sherlock Holmes's dog that did not bark in the night. Even with the recognition of Levi as an important writer beyond his own time and place, slight effort has been made to locate him in literary or cultural topography more generally, to reflect on where he stands in the broad spectrum of writers and thinkers ranging from lyric poets celebrating the self through the varieties of fiction and drama and into the varied world of discursive, ostensibly nonfiction writing.[19] Almost certainly, the hesitation to consider Levi in these terms reflects his choice of the Holocaust as one of his large concerns, a sense that the uniqueness often attributed to that event would be undermined by placing or comparing its representations among or with others; to this would be added the awkwardness and potential danger of placing writings about the Holocaust fully on one side or the other of the honorific if contested divide between fiction and nonfiction. Examples of these complexities are plentiful, not only for "memoirs" like that of Benjamin Wilkomirski, which appeared first as a fearsome historical autobiography but then turned out to be, literally, manufactured—thus opening the question for many readers of exactly how much difference the shift in those categories actually makes—but also for texts moving in the other direction, like Elie Wiesel's *Night*, which in its original Yiddish and even its first redacted versions in French and English was identified as a novel but has found its way currently into the categories of nonfiction and memoir.

As likely a reason as any of these, however, is the difficulty of assigning Levi's work to any of the standard genres or categories, even within the broad outlines of fiction or nonfiction. This seems itself a clue as to where he ought to be placed, since there are representatives of one distinguished literary tradition in particular that have encountered similar difficulties and for at least some of the same reasons. This is the company of moralist or edifying writers—figures like Montaigne and Thoreau, Pascal and Aesop, Emerson, Camus, Orwell. Significantly, the now professionalized fields of learning and criticism find it difficult to place these authors and others like them within the categories recognized in the standard university organization of "departments": Is there a place in that organization for commentators? critics? essayists? belle-lettrists? Objections are plentiful to each of these; there seems always much more space *between* the standard rubrics than within them. But more than any other feature, there remains the unifying and common thread among the authors mentioned and their kind, of their insistence on speaking about the human without privileging any particular one of the aspects to be found there: looking at each human being, each person, as if that person were indeed a whole— front, side, back, inside and outside. The professionalization of disciplines has drawn lines stressing partiality, fragmentation; and although this tendency to categorize is defensible in its own terms, what it leads to cannot then claim comprehensiveness. That such compartmentalization blocks out nuances that shade away from their individual emphases explains the difficulty of finding a particular space in this topography for writers in the group mentioned—with whom Levi has an evident affinity specifically because he is not only a survivor-writer or a Jewish writer or a scientist-writer. He is surely each of these, but none by itself, and even the several together do not do him justice. Levi did write at least one "Holocaust novel"—but he also wrote at least one "non-Holocaust novel"; in addition, he wrote memoirs, reflective essays, and criticism, all of them contributing cumulatively to his standing as a writer and thinker. What emerges here is a literary scaffolding built around a structure of stubborn historical and scientific facts, with the whole animated by a search for what is significantly human in that variety—the human for which differences among the facts, including their extremities (for better and worse) are as relevant for understanding the human subject as are the norms that also apply equally and equably to them all, together with the extremities and eccentricities that turn out to be almost as common.

But this is precisely the assembly of human elements—*their* periodic table—that has given continued life to the moralist tradition of the writers mentioned and among whom Levi should be placed. Their illumination continues despite the challenge to them by what have become the conventional lines of professional separation. Their writings, with Levi's now to be added to the list, demand attention even at a time when reading at leisure—reading not for information or diversion but as deliberation—contends for a place within an impatient society with little leisure for leisure that often seems distraught in encounters with anything lacking the quick edge of immediacy. The gathering of authors mentioned is distinguished: distinguished first in their by-now classical standing, but also by the effort required to establish the common category which they have created—not, of course, for the sake of defining still another category or specialty but to assure other future writers of a possible home.

Time will undoubtedly tell more about Levi's position within this group than we are now able to tell, but an additional standard, of invidious difference, is more immediately applicable to him than the yet-to-be-tested standard of historical sur-

vival. This involves asking who among Levi's contemporary—or up to this time, his successor—writers has presented to readers the issues or events he addressed as evocatively and generatively as he did. It seems not only just but necessary to scrutinize Levi in this way precisely because the network of events and issues which he took as his subject have occasioned an imposing surfeit of writing: the Holocaust, human nature, science, culture. One test here for the community of moralists who have been mentioned is whether *they* would recognize and welcome Levi as one of them. That he was not predictable in the way of his writing increases rather than detracts from the probability of how that decision would go; who, after all, would have predicted the ways taken by Montaigne or Thoreau? One overriding condition that Levi's writings meet in their relationship to the writings of the moralist tradition is that they speak so often, variously, and inventively about the fact that practice in life *matters*. A principle that Levi himself also practiced.

4

The Jewish Question

"I was turned into a Jew by others."
—Primo Levi, interview with Edith Bruck,
Il Messaggero, 1976

"Until these months [of 1938] it had not
meant much to me that I was a Jew. Within
myself, and in my contacts with my Christian
friends, I had always considered my origin as an
almost negligible but curious fact: a small amusing
anomaly, like having a crooked nose or freckles."
—Primo Levi, *The Periodic Table*, 1975

"If it hadn't been for the racial laws and
the concentration camps, I'd probably no longer
be a Jew, except for my last name."
—Primo Levi, interview with Ferdinando Camon,
in *Conversations with Primo Levi*, 1987

IN 1938 the Jewish communities in Italy numbered approximately fifty thousand in a national populace of 44 million, not much more than one-tenth of one percent. Over the centuries of Jewish settlement in Italy, beginning in the South during Roman times and in the North mainly after the fifteenth-century expulsion of Jews from the Iberian Peninsula, there had been assimilation by conversion and intermarriage, but little of those practices in the early twentieth century stemmed from overt legal or political pressures. Jewish community members had achieved public recognition and high office usually without reference to their Jewish origins: in the armed forces, in the national Senate, in academic positions. What would have been exceptional in other western and still more in eastern European countries or the United States passed almost without public notice in Italy. When Primo Levi writes, then, that when growing up, his being Jewish was an "almost negligible but curious fact," that recollection did not mean that he was oblivious to the atmosphere in his schools or social contacts; he might have been speaking for the Jewish community at large, certainly for the comfortable middle class of which his own family was a part. In retrospect, that community's political acculturation may appear most striking. Mussolini's rise to power in 1922 found support even then within the Jewish community, several hundred of whose members joined the Fascists' march on Rome. In 1938, more than a third of Italy's Jewish adults (about ten thousand)—including Cesare, Primo's father—were members of the Fascist Party. To be sure, after the adoption of the anti-Jewish legislation in that year, those members were forced out of the Party, although even then many of them foresaw no more severe measures in the offing. That the Levi family in Turin still felt "at home," as suggested in the epigraphs opening this chapter, can then be taken at face value—certainly for Levi's own consciousness, transgenerational as it must have been: the *difference* of being Jewish in the comings and goings of everyday life seemed to him in recollection to have had little weight.

Independent evidence, however, and still other statements by Levi himself, reported as they are in his reflections postwar, indicate that this account of his early sense of Jewish identity represents (as how could it not?) the harsh influence and contrast of that wartime experience as compared with what had preceded it. At the very least, the denial of earlier significance of his Jewish identity is, on the basis of his own evidence, exaggerated: in strict historical terms, misleading or, to put the matter more bluntly, mistaken. The effects of being Jewish for Levi after Auschwitz would understandably be sharper, more severe, than any he had previously encountered. But this does not mean that his sense of that identity before Auschwitz was as vague as he depicts it, and the exaggeration in this contrast becomes clear in a number of his own descriptions of his early family life. Those descriptions, also written or reported post-Auschwitz, include substantial details of what it meant for Levi to grow up in his extended Piedmont Jewish (*emphatically* Jewish) family in the 1920s and 1930s: the vivid presence of a strong Jewish influence, at once openly practiced and as unconscious in the atmosphere as the currency of everyday language inevitably is, was evident and lasting.

This apparent conflict in witness-memory—in effect, Levi vs. Levi—may seem incongruous. When Levi reports in 1980 on his sense of identity of forty-five years earlier, emphasizing the irrelevance at that time of his Jewish identity, it may seem impossible to contest those assertions even on the evidence of conflicting statements he made at about the same time concerning the detail and texture of his everyday life that would have had a part in that sense of identity. Do not all reports about one's self-identity have the force of "privileged access," of undeniability? The statement "I feel warm" even expressed in a cold place is not open to dispute or correction: the speaker may be ill and feverish but would not be judged "mistaken." Accounts of *past* feelings, however, pass through the filter of intervening events between the past and present and the effect they often have on memory's shapes and proportions. And the latter cross-current seems clearly to bring out the contrast between Levi's claim of the minimal difference defined by Jewish identity early in his consciousness and his other descriptions, also later and externally observed, of that same Jewish family life. For when he writes in *The Periodic Table* and in other, less systematic accounts about the atmosphere in which he grew up, the presence of a pervasive Jewish character becomes much more compelling than the epigraphs at the beginning of this chapter would allow for. The claim of having been "turned into a Jew by others" exemplifies this. On the face of it, what this statement asserts applies to some extent to every child's experience of his or her later Jewish (or any other religious or ethnic) identity; in this sense, although Levi's implied reference is to the extraordinary persecution and danger he later experienced, the generalization he bases on it obscures a more common ground of identity. Admittedly, the concept of an "atmosphere," familial or cultural, is vague—but hardly more so than reference to the *physical* atmosphere. Few people are conscious of breathing as meeting specific biological and physical conditions, let alone as an act—that is, until a breakdown occurs. It is not that such a breakdown *must* occur before the awareness may dawn, although just that claim has at times been invoked as the initiating source of Jewish self-identity. (In his *Anti-Semite and the Jew*, for example, Jean-Paul Sartre claims antisemitism as not only an influence on but an originary source of Jewish identity—as if that identity would not otherwise have emerged: a flagrant anachronism.)

Levi's recollections of his childhood and the family members who inhabited it, especially his account of his own activities—his two-year preparations for his bar mitzvah and

his commitment then, fleeting as it would prove, to lay tefil-
lin (phylacteries) daily—are undoubtedly colored by the same
literary imagination that would be fashioning his fictional
or quasi-fictional writings by the time *The Periodic Table* appeared (1975), but the specific historical inlay of Jewish identity in these references is nonetheless unmistakable. When he
writes in "Argon," the opening chapter of *The Periodic Table*,
that his family resembled that element: "inert," "noble," and
"rare"—each of those qualities is linked to evidence of the family's Piedmont Jewish past as much as to some of their notable individual idiosyncrasies that caught the author's literary
eye. When his "Uncle" Bramin surrenders to his parents' opposition to his marrying the "goya" whom they had hired as
a maid, he takes to his bed for the next twenty-two years but
then, after the parents' death, marries her anyway; the family opposition here was clearly at least as much sectarian as it
was personal, however distant from orthodox religious practice
the family members otherwise were. Even as Levi recalls his
own father's expressions of guilt when buying and eating the
forbidden prosciutto he craved, the youth's impression would
be significant, as he recalls his father "watching me out of the
corner of his eye as if he feared my judgment or hoped for my
complicity." The Piedmont-Jewish dialect which according to
Levi's account never had more than several thousand speak-
ers was distinctive enough in its evocation of Hebrew roots for
him to recall and identify at least some of the features, including such slang uses as that of the Hebrew *ruach* (wind or spirit)
for "fart." He himself appears as a figure in the chapter "Zinc"
as the (Jewish) "impurity," the seed of difference required by
zinc, otherwise a stolid and "boring" element, in order for it to
be set in motion—that is, to produce a reaction from it.

Even assuming the role of literary embellishment in these
narratives, there is no reason to think that they were spun out
of whole cloth and much reason to lean toward the contrary.

Certainly the material was not only clearly enough defined in memory to serve as the writer's source but explicit enough in exhibiting Levi's Jewish roots to disclose them as quite the opposite of meaningless or trivial. He makes no claim in the narratives for their effect on him as an adult or as the writer who is then recounting them; but the narrative speaks for itself, as authoritative a representation of Levi's early sense of Jewish identity as the conflicting one he also claimed retrospectively, in which the presence of Auschwitz may seem more basically, even exclusively, determinant.

Again, none of these qualifying recollections or descriptions diminishes the impact that Levi's "war" had on him. If anything, the detail and emotional force of these recollections underscore the war's impact on his sense of Jewish identity and particularity; its effect, then, was less to create than to bring into sharper focus the divided consciousness that Levi would eventually ascribe not only to himself but to modern Jewish identity in the Diaspora as such: a feature of the Jewish condition—as both a description of and an answer to the Jewish Question—that he came to regard as suitable for Diaspora Jews who then (and now) made up a majority of the world Jewish populace. This "answer" to the Jewish Question appears on a much smaller but exemplarily concrete scale in Levi's explanation of his selection from Sholem Aleichem's Tevye stories in *The Search for Roots*, his anthology of writings that remained significant for him. His introductory comments to the Sholem Aleichem selection depict Tevye not in the standard monochrome of a shtetl Jew—the ironic Yiddish wit in a framework of biblical quotation—but as claiming a place on a broader and to some extent conflicting canvas. So, as Levi put it, "In his own way, Tevye senses the fracture that divides the world, he is himself sadly divided: in so far as he is a Jew of the Diaspora his destiny is to be wrenched in two."[1] "*Wrenched*"—though at the same time very much alive in the world. And if *Tevye* the *milchiker*, the shtetl dairyman, can represent the Diaspora Jew in his divided consciousness, Levi's own sense of a divided identity—the particularist Jew in opposition to the encroaching representations of a secular world—becomes still more vividly defined and present.

Again, Levi's recollections of self and family in his youth could hardly be expected to stand out as sharply in memory as the persecution and hardship he experienced from 1938 on. When, echoing a friend, he reports that "Auschwitz was a university for me," he is speaking about a large expanse of *Jewish* learning almost as formidable as the other serious lessons he learned there. Auschwitz brought his first encounter with Yiddish as the mother tongue (the *mame-loshon*) of the majority of European Jews; it was also his first sustained encounter with religiously observant Jews for whom a commitment to God's rule, his goodness and justice, remained steadfast in the face of what Levi found in the Lager to be the strongest possible counterevidence to those attributes. Even before 1938, he reports, he had sympathized with the Zionist ideal of a homeland for Jews in Palestine, though without much knowledge of either the movement or the land, and certainly with no sense of the urgency he noted and in good measure agreed with after the war for those survivors who placed Zionism at the center of all Jewish aspirations. That the reality of a Jewish homeland might have blunted if not averted the Nazis' attempt at extermination became for Levi, initially at least, one of the "lessons" taught by Auschwitz. The diversity of Jews he encountered there—intermingled from Greece, France, Poland, from Germany itself—caused him to reflect on the Italian-Jewish community and *its* ways; thus too, of course, on his own place and identity in relation to his fellow Häftlinge. Before Auschwitz, he had had a university education in chemistry; what he learned in the Lager brought him knowledge of a subject he had previously not imagined to exist.

All these lessons remained with the Primo Levi who, returning to Turin in 1945, felt the urgent need to recount his experience in the Lager and who, impelled by that, began to write *If This Is a Man;* who then also took up his career as a chemist; who married Lucia Morpurgo, daughter of a family with a more assertive sense of Jewish identity than that of the Levi household; and for whom as a consequence of the war, "being Jewish" had shifted from something presumptive, on the edge of consciousness and will, to a place close to the center of his self-identity. This did not mean that Levi became more observant religiously; if anything, the hold of religious practice on him and later on his own household became weaker over time than it had been in his youth. So, for example, he recounts defensively the decision that had been made to send his two young children to Jewish (private) elementary schools: "With the full agreement of my wife, we sent our children to Jewish elementary school to counterbalance the pressure of the dominant Catholic culture around them, but after that we pressed to move them into state schools." And at the same time, in response to a question about his and his adult household's observance of Jewish customs or adherence to doctrine, he was forthright and unequivocal: "No, nothing." "It's as if my religious sense has been amputated. . . . I constructed a Jewish culture for myself, but very late, after the War."[2]

Here again, however, Levi also serves as witness against himself. Would it have been only accidental (or a matter of his own inexperience) that in 1947, having returned to the social upheaval of postwar Italy, Levi married a woman whose family was firmly lodged in the Turin Jewish community? Lucia's father had taught literature at the liceo attended by Levi; after his dismissal from that position because of the racial laws, he taught at and then became principal of the Hebrew school that the community established for Jewish students; he performed the marriage, under the chuppah, between Primo and

Lucia. Primo's mother (née Luzzati) was herself the daughter of a fabric merchant in the solid upper-middle-class Turin Jewish community, and if Primo's father, Cesare, an engineer who traveled and worked outside of Turin on several occasions, was more worldly and secular than these and his other forebears, the sense of historical identity traced in Levi family lore to smaller towns of the Piedmont region remained substantial, and not only because of the indelible and recognizable family name.

Undeniable as such roots were, consciously and unconsciously religious doctrine and practice stood increasingly at the periphery of the family's identity, but this tendency needs to be understood as becoming common not only in the Levi milieu of Turin but in the variations and evolution of European Jewish self-identity from the nineteenth century on: the distinction between culture and religion which, though debated constantly at the same time that it was expanding its reach, became a familiar phenomenon with odd and unpredictable turns. (In a different national but parallel social setting, Gershom Scholem writes in his autobiography that as a teenager, he received a grudging Christmas present from his parents in the form of a photograph of Theodor Herzl.) However strong the cultural pull away from religious practice, there was never any doubt or wavering for Levi in his own cultural identity of its incorporation into and dependence on its Jewish sources. Of course, some of these were imposed later by force, but even then his regard for them and what he constructed on his understanding of them reflected his own affirmation. That he had been sent to Auschwitz *as* a Jew was never far from his consciousness; that those selected for the gas chambers were sent to their deaths as Jews would be a constant shadow. And that he himself survived *despite* the fate prescribed for him as a Jew by the Nazis, a fate which would have ensured that neither he nor any other Jew would remain alive, was also clear to him. His own survival as well as that of any others, he said repeatedly, was due almost entirely to chance and luck—and if there are few lives in which such factors do not have some role, their decisiveness in Levi's history was nonetheless unusual. Furthermore, whether as consequence or echo, this pattern between a divided Jewish and non-Jewish presence continued through the forty postwar years of his life: detachment on one hand, commitment on the other. Thus, he married, worked as a chemist in the secular community of SIVA, raised two children who would grow up in middle-class Turin—with the family remaining formally members of Turin's Jewish community, registered in the municipality as Jewish, and paying dues (taxes) to the community of which the Turin synagogue and its staff were principal beneficiaries—at the same time that he was venturing in his writings and friendships into a nondenominational world.

Levi's first two books drew largely Jewish audiences at first (this was most clearly evident outside Italy, to a lesser degree in Italy itself because of community's limited numbers), but the circle of his audience as his writings turned in other directions acquired a much broader circumference. On the two trips he made outside Europe, to Israel in 1968 and to the United States in 1985, he was discomfited to find himself, especially in the latter setting, presented (and questioned) as a *Jewish* writer. At one point in his U.S. trip, as if worn down by the repetition of that designation, he professed to accept it and wrote an essay to that effect—but even then he clearly hoped for a more general category that would acknowledge his second profession, after chemistry, as that of a *writer*, with the role of Jewish writer subsidiary to that. In this reluctance he placed the same emphasis and for similar reasons as those that spurred the resistance of several other contemporary "Jewish" writers like Saul Bellow and Philip Roth to the designation, although they too experienced indifferent success in this effort. In addition to his personal reasons for this resistance, Levi was well aware of the difficulty of defining what (or who) a Jewish writer was, even for critics or readers who attached weight or faith to the category. Biological, racial, or even ethnic criteria have their own obvious and severe problems; Jewish "themes" or writing about experience from a Jewish "perspective" pose similar difficulties. Jewish humor? Irony, a strong element in humor more generally, was a favorite impulse of Levi's, one he brought into the open even when he was writing about Auschwitz. But the serious uses to which irony can be put are as common in literary history as they are significant, notably clear in archetypical literary figures like Sophocles and Shakespeare. A variety of jokes that Levi favored have been recorded, some of them related to the Jewish Question itself. So, for example: An antisemite is berating a Jewish neighbor, evidently not for the first time, with the charge of deicide—the responsibility of Jews (thus, also of *this* Jew) for the crucifixion and death of Jesus. Finally, after the antisemite is unconvinced by several rebuttals, the Jew responds impatiently: "Okay, okay, so we killed him—but, after all, it was only for three days." Humor? Yes—and surely indicative of Levi's taste. But Jewish? Why? It cannot be because it is about a Jew (more precisely, about two of them). At some near point, the conclusion begins to emerge that in looking to "Jewish" as a *literary* category, the flame is hardly worth the candle.[3]

But if the question of Levi's identification as a "Jewish writer" seems problematic conceptually or practically, the same cannot be said about the issue of his Jewish identity; complex as that issue also is, not only are the stakes there higher, but the evidence is more compelling. That the Italian racial laws of 1938 had an impact on Levi's sense of identity—as for Italian Jews generally—is indisputable; his later months as a partisan, his capture, and then his deportation to Auschwitz underscored that identity much more forcefully. But, as proposed earlier, in the accounts he gives of his family life from his childhood memories and encounters, in the family lore, some of which no doubt he came to know only after he had left the house but which continued to frame his childhood recollections, the atmosphere is dense with practices, events, and emotional associations that mark it off vividly from what would have appeared at the same time in Italian non-Jewish homes and family memories. Perhaps his family history and life also differed from other *Italian-Jewish* settings, but they also certainly differed from those in the homes and family lore of his non-Jewish friends and acquaintances, of whose practices the young Levi would have been as unknowing as they were of his.

Yet balanced against this tacit "given" of Jewish identity, Levi's schoolmates in his formal education and his other non-Jewish acquaintances added a conflicting element—a clash about which he himself seemed at the time not fully aware. In this identity, he appeared as a comfortably middle-class student in a sophisticated Italian city with broad cultural and social traditions. His formal education took place entirely under Mussolini's Fascist government, but enough remained institutionally even then of the classical (and elitist) education of the Italian educational system to allow for, even to sustain his secular and universalist interests. At least in retrospect, he saw his early and continuing preference for "materialist" science and chemistry as a political and moral reaction against the Fascist advocacy of a version of "spirit," a concept which struck Levi as beyond the reach of all scientific evidence. (The principal Fascist theorists arguing for the latter were Giovanni Gentile and the young Benedetto Croce, who later modified if he did not entirely reverse his views on this, at least on the racial question.) It is worth noting that Levi's commitment here did not focus on fascism's emerging racist elements in Italy which, despite their often brutal consequences, were nonetheless less deeply and systematically embedded than in Nazi Germany. Elements of this racism were certainly present and at times linked to Italian nationalism; they clearly intensified the brutality evident in Italy's invasion of Ethiopia and then later in the Salo government's treatment of the Jews after the Germans took over in 1943. Indeed, even after the war, Levi accepted the then conventional view of color-coded racial distinctions, although he was skeptical of some of the basic generalizations about racial differences and specifically about anything like a systematic racial hierarchy. More important in terms of his own personal development, he recognized that even under fascism, he was able to make his way to an alternate mode of thinking, though he recognized at the same time that some of Italy's best-known scientists found no incompatibility between science and fascism. Science, in other words, might have been opposed to fascism in principle, as Levi held, but it did not provide immunity from it. That Levi was an unusually gifted student undoubtedly helped him in sustaining this critical sense, as well as in managing his academic career without taking on the role of a public rebel or dissenter, as some of his contemporaries did. This superficial harmony undoubtedly added to the effect of the emerging division in his identity as virtually invisible, akin to a line of longitude: unseen but real, with a steady balance between the two sides—until an external and unavoidable source of conflict came between them.

The anti-Jewish legislation of 1938 served as precisely such a source, a formal shock to the system which struck the Jewish community as startling despite the earlier signs that might have been interpreted as foreshadowing. The Lateran Treaties of 1929, in which Mussolini, among other stipulations, recognized Roman Catholicism as the state religion, would in retrospect have served as one such sign; the 1933 Concordat between the Nazi government and the Vatican in which the Vatican, in exchange for "ecclesiastical" freedom, agreed to refrain in Germany from political action would have been another. And after 1933, the signs included reports that began to reach Italy of Nazi actions and ideological extremities that struck more deeply than anything experienced or anticipated at the time in Italy. For all but a few Italian Jews, the very extremity of those reports, including, if only symbolically, events like the systematic public book burnings in major German academic centers in April 1933, served to strain credulity. The division in Levi's sense of identity between the thread of Jewish identity and that of the humanist and scientist—the Enlightenment man—was by then embedded, but the division thus marked was still, at least superficially, a peaceable one.

This apparent coexistence broke down, however, in ways already discussed which Levi succinctly summarizes in the chapter "Gold" in *The Periodic Table:* "'They' had declared 'us' different, and different 'we' would be."[4] The divided—different—sense of identity that explicitly emerged then would never attain its former quiescence or harmony after that. This does not mean that Levi found himself seriously troubled by it. Even *after* Auschwitz, Levi seemed to find a solution for it akin to the medieval "double theory" of truth—interpreting what he regarded as valuable on each side of the divide as compatible with the other because the *criteria* for judging each were also different: the particularism of Jewish cultural history consistent with the universalist theoretical principles of science. For doctrinal truth, science was the arbiter; for cultural and social identity, the Jewish tradition was significant, though even then, because of the rich Italian cultural presence, not exclusively.

A symbolic—also literal—indicator of this division appears in Levi's attitude toward Palestine and later Israel, after the state's independence in 1948. According to his own account, Levi had early been drawn to Zionist ideals: "From 1935 to 1940 I was fascinated by Zionist propaganda, I admired the country it described and the future it was planning, equality and fraternity."[5] The importance he attached to that land or state became more intense with his wartime experience in Auschwitz and his

post-liberation months in Poland and Russia because of his encounters there with other Displaced Persons. He was affected
in these meetings not only by survivors who were Zionists of
long standing, but by the larger number of survivors for whom
Palestine was the only potential refuge to which they could
turn. Many of the latter thus became Zionists *faute de mieux;*
they might have preferred to emigrate elsewhere or even to
return to their former homes, but they were aware of the difficulties of arranging the former and, through reports of postwar
hostility that included pogroms in some of their hometowns,
of the dangers of the other. It is worth noting that even during the eleven-month period between Levi's liberation and his
homecoming, when he was still ignorant of what he would find
remaining of his family and home in Turin, he does not report
considering Palestine as a personal option. Indeed, he did not
seem to have considered any other alternative either—this despite the fact that his father and his father's two brothers had
bought property in Brazil before the war. Levi's indifference
might have changed if he had found greater disruption than he
did upon his return to Turin, but it is also indicative of the extent to which Levi identified with his native place.

Levi's positive view of a prospective Jewish homeland, if
only in principle, was and has remained the attitude of a majority of Jews in the Diaspora: a sense of attachment in Diaspora Jewish communities to Palestine and later Israel that was
not viewed as conflicting with a settled life elsewhere. In this
regard, as the prospect of a Jewish state became increasingly
likely, and even with the awareness of the Holocaust's enormity and the related vulnerability felt by many in Jewish Diaspora communities, Levi found himself continuing to move
steadily toward a conception of the Jewish "Diaspora" that he
had already anticipated: attachment to the principle of a Jewish
homeland that did not entail a commitment to emigrate or live
there.

This attitude of Levi's persisted also after the immediate pressure of postwar resettlement and Israel's War of Independence in 1948 diminished, in part but not only because of the continuing struggles that beset the new state. So, for example, he joined in public expressions of solidarity and concern at the prospect of war with Egypt in spring 1967; with many others, he viewed the circumstances as a threat to Israel's existence. His corresponding sense of relief at the outcome of the Six-Day War in June led not long afterward to his single visit to Israel. This occurred in March 1968 as one of a group of some forty Italian former members of the Liberty and Justice partisan groups. (It is relevant to note that the Rosselli brothers, Carlo and Nello, founders of the Liberty and Justice movement and murdered by Fascist agents in 1937, were, as Socialists and antinationalists, also early and outspoken anti-Zionists.) The trip to Israel lasted about a week and included tours both in the north of the newly occupied Golan Heights bordering Syria and in the south of the Sinai battlefields, with carnage from the war still visible on those two fronts. It also brought Levi into contact with features of Israeli culture on which he commented as thin and (unfavorably) different from what he saw as his own Italian and European values. The latter may have reflected something of Levi's personal resentment, later expressed more explicitly, at the lack of interest he found in Israel in his own writing about the Holocaust; after much ambivalence earlier within Israel of public regard for the Holocaust and even for its survivor-immigrants, the event was then in the process of becoming a significant feature of Israel's "civil religion," but at the time Levi's writings had virtually no presence there. (A Hebrew translation of *If This Is a Man* did not appear until 1989.)

In any event, Levi was no more inclined after his visit than previously to consider emigration to Israel; if anything, the visit strengthened his view of the viability of the Jewish Diaspora and even of its importance for sustaining Israel itself, a role reversal to that envisioned by traditional Zionism. "The role of Israel as the unifying center for Judaism now—and I emphasize the word 'now'—is in eclipse. So the center of gravity of the Jewish world must turn back, must move out of Israel and back into the Diaspora."[6] Levi made the latter statement in 1984, mainly in reaction to what he regarded as the course taken then by Israel's political and cultural policies, but it reflected not only specific misgivings about those policies but his own growing assurance of the viability of Jewish existence in the Diaspora—certainly for him personally, but also for the other communities he had observed—as well perhaps as a sense of the vulnerability to which the State of Israel itself seemed subject. Again, this view from the perspective of the Diaspora was not uncommon either at the time or since; it was intensified for Levi by his generally antinationalist political ideals and moral humanism that he felt increasingly to conflict with what he regarded as growing nationalist tendencies within Israel.

Levi's reservations about these issues were epitomized for him in the 1977 Israeli elections which brought the Herut Party to power, with its leader, Menachem Begin (whose own history as leader of the Irgun was familiar to Levi, as were also earlier interactions between the Jabotinsky Revisionists and Italian Fascists), installed as prime minister. The consequences of that political shift from the socialist-democratic past of the Israeli political landscape were for Levi further sharpened by Israel's invasion of Lebanon in 1982, especially as its extent moved beyond the goals initially announced as its justification. Even at the war's inception, Levi had signed a proclamation sponsored by a group of Italian intellectuals which decried the invasion. As events evolved, Begin himself would be misled about the war's course; the Kahan Commission that later investigated policies and acts during the war placed ultimate responsibil-

ity on Begin and his defense minister, Ariel Sharon, concluding that the massacres in the Lebanese refugee camps of Sabra
and Shatila, though perpetrated by Lebanese Falangist forces,
had required and received the acquiescence of the Israeli military command. Following the massacres but before the Kahan
Commission report, Levi spoke up in a sharply worded interview published in *La Repubblica* (titled "Begin Should Go")
calling for the resignations of Begin and Sharon. Both those
resignations would eventually occur, but even then as a result
of pressures and procedures that did not, in Levi's view, respond to the central moral issues that had been raised.

Levi's reaction to Israel's political direction in the war would
shape his views for the remaining four years of his life, surfacing, for example, in a series of interviews that were among the
last he gave, published in 1987 by Ferdinando Camon as *Conversations with Primo Levi.* Thus, Levi's statement that "Israel is
taking on the nature and behavior of its neighbors. I say it with
sorrow and anger."[7] And he reacted along similar lines to criticism that surfaced in some of his public appearances during his
trip to the United States in the spring of 1985. He found himself uncomfortable in a number of the appearances which had
been arranged for largely Jewish audiences (he asked only half-
jokingly at one of these events in New York City whether there
were any New York residents who were *not* Jewish) to whom
he was presented as a "Jewish" writer. As mentioned, he finally
if grudgingly surrendered to the label; he even spoke in one of
his lectures about what it meant *to be* a Jewish writer. But then,
too, he found himself challenged at times for his views on Israel
which were known—critically—to some among his audiences.
Perhaps because he had not expected such challenges, perhaps
hindered by having to speak and respond to questions publicly
in English, also no doubt because of his strong feelings on the
issues, Levi spoke more forthrightly than some of his audiences
were willing to hear. One such evening in Brooklyn had to be

concluded because of the uproar following a comment by Levi that perhaps Israel as a state had been a historical mistake.

Again, the importance of such occurrences for understanding Levi's view of his Jewish identity is the division it reveals within Levi's commitments: on one hand, a personal and emotional attachment to a culture (in relation to Israel, including the land) that he recognized as part not only of his own genealogy but also of his present; on the other hand, a commitment to values that were for him trans- or even supracultural. That these two attachments might at times clash is more relevant for understanding Levi's view of them than any question about which of the two sides was (or should have been) more basic for him. If somehow forced to *choose* between them, much in Levi's life and work suggests that he would have inclined to the universal and supracultural values over the other; but that choice was not forced on him, and he was thus able to sustain both, on his own terms in each case and with both commitments subject to the same skepticism and awareness of historical contingency that motivated so much of his thinking and doing—all this in addition to the remarkable curiosity reflected in his writing that would find openings and reversals in even the slightest natural or historical events.

A distinctive example of this range and hierarchy of motifs appeared in some formal comments that Levi made in 1984 on the occasion of the centenary of the Turin synagogue and of Turin Jewish communal life. After a brief review of the way the community had sustained itself, indeed had flourished despite its relatively small numbers, Levi turned to its position (and his own) in the present, finding then that the vividness and force of that communal past appeared to him to be in decline: "There exists for every human group a critical mass, below which stability ceases; at that point it tends toward an even more excessive dilution and toward a silent and painless dissolution. Our community, except for unforeseeable events, seems to have started down this road."[8] These words seemed to combine elegy with eulogy. Composed within two years of his death, they hinted at what Levi saw as one part of his own history being submerged by a second part (though Levi would not necessarily have *chosen* this), a movement of history in which questions of justice were also ultimately dependent on constraints that the actual imposed on what was possible, where even human history with all its innovative power of decision and imagination gave way to the constraints of natural history. Did this apparent leave-taking side with the universal over the particular or with the particular over the universal? Again, Levi does not seem here to be expressing a *preference*. Whatever else irony is or is not, it is clearly nondenominational; that in itself goes some way toward explaining Levi's continuing and final commitment to it.

In all that has been said, then, the question lingers of exactly how important Levi's willed Jewish sense of identity was for him: the bottom line, after all, of the Jewish Question, whether posed individually or collectively, for anyone with a Jewish past or present. That Levi's personal history took unusual turns even in a historical framework intimately familiar with unusual turns clearly complicates an already complex question. Would he have become a writer at all if he had not been Jewish, if he had not been singled out *as* Jewish in the way that he was initially by Mussolini's regime and then by Hitler's? At different times, he himself gave contradictory answers to this question, as he did also to the question of his status as a Jewish writer—at least sometimes suggesting that he might well have become a writer in any event. All of Levi's attachments spread widely and deeply; interests could not be authentic for him without a committed personal investment. That his Jewish identity became over time more important for him than it would have under "ordinary" circumstances is certain, but then too, even ordinary circumstances often reveal themselves as more than ordinary; only a moment is required. What is

Levi among students. As he had written in the poem "Shema": "I commend these words to you . . . / Repeat them to your children."

undeniable is that that identity *was* important in his life. More important than other factors? More important than some others? than all others? To choose among these, one would have to know more than anyone, including Levi himself, could possibly know or have known; even before that, it assumes that the answer would shed light that nothing else had or could—which in a figure like Levi seems itself as likely to be contentious as the issue it would hope to resolve.

5

Thinking

"Above all I contracted the habit of
never remaining indifferent to the individuals
that chance brings before me."
—Primo Levi, *The Drowned and the Saved*, 1989

"I know with my hands and my nose, with
my senses, like any naïve realist."
—Primo Levi, interview with
Germaine Greer, 1985, in *The Voice of Memory*

"Evolution has always proved itself
to be enormously more intelligent than
the best evolutionists."
—Primo Levi, "Inventing an Animal,"
Other People's Trades, 1989

PRIMO LEVI was by education and profession first a chemist, and he brought that background to bear on his second, later profession of writer, engaging both lines of work simultaneously for thirty years with the only strain between them during those years, in his own words, being the pressure of time. He did not in either of the two commitments consider himself a philosopher, and indeed he expressed impatience with the abstractions of traditional philosophy and its contrivance of technical terms when so many more pressing and concrete human issues demanded attention. Although he read widely in six languages and in other literatures through translation, referring often in writing and conversation to a range of authors, he rarely mentions the canonical figures of philosophy. He did not consider himself a professional historian either, but by contrast his interest there was sophisticated and constant. In part this was impelled by events in his own history, but history as such had a vividness for him that only an unusual eye for detail and a mind searching for connections and causal explanations could realize. In putting these impulses to work, he came to know as much about the structure and process of the "Final Solution" as almost all his contemporaries and as much as many professional historians. (Historical errors that appear in his writings, like the exaggerated number [four million] he at one time cites of those killed in Auschwitz, reflect the state of knowledge at the time.) And this same focus, sharpened by personal experience—motivated also by a concurrent drive for historical understanding—came to extend beyond the Holocaust to broader aspects of cultural and natural history as well.

This multifaceted interest in history also led Levi beyond it. For he realized, as the most incisive historians have, that even detailed historical descriptions may still fail to provide understanding or explanation of the events to which they call attention: the pieces joined in historical narrative often raise questions and assume answers that go beyond the narrative's own grounds, pushing historical accounts into an area that is more than "only" historical. Unlike many writers who reach this point and then carry on either by fiat or by cutting the discussion short, however, Levi consistently followed those steps over the border and into territory marked off—vaguely, but nonetheless—as philosophy.

In this sense, Levi appears as something like a "natural" philosopher, combining an intuition of significant theoretical questions underpinning historical practice with a keen sense of where responses to them can (*or* cannot) be found. And he applies the results of both those abilities as cogently as many professional philosophers do—not only the considerable number who regard history as largely irrelevant to their work, but also those who accept its relevance, which turns out often to be acceptance more in principle than in practice. (The very notion of "professional" philosophy has itself, after all, been brief in comparison to its lengthy "nonprofessional" past, which reaches from Socrates to Spinoza.) As a further distinction, Levi tested the conclusions he reached and advocated not in the standard formal framework of argument and counterargument but in specific historical contexts of which the Holocaust was a principal but not the exclusive one, assessing his conclusions, then, against that unified background of evidence. He applied these tests, moreover, without placing himself rather than the issues at the center of his account—resisting a temptation that often overcomes writers not only of memoirs or autobiographies but also of larger and supposedly impersonal historical narratives. He himself introduces the Greek term *phronesis*—"practical wisdom" in contrast to theory—as a goal to which he was committed.

One might here risk an analogy between Levi's writing and Nietzsche's view of the "gay" (or "happy," *Fröhliche*) "science," the idea of digging beneath conceptual superstructures in order to demonstrate the connection between life and thought:

thought, in other words, as practice. In one of the epigraphs to this chapter, Levi, when asked how he knew what he knew, responded by citing the knowledge he acquired through the senses; he would later link that with an emphasis on the difference between "learning something" (knowing the facts) and "learning how to do something," as in the knowledge of a craftsman. The comparison to Nietzsche here is in other respects a stretch; on the few occasions that Levi specifically mentions Nietzsche, he criticizes his oracular and bombastic style. But a corroborative basis for the comparison and an important clue to the nature of Levi's thinking is the genealogy in which Levi comments that he would single out Rabelais as his literary father: Rabelais, at once the transgressive and the comic, who "knows human misery, [but is] a good physician also who when he writes . . . wants to heal it."[1]

Levi's philosophy or thinking can be categorized in various ways, but my focus here is on five topics that have significant roles in his writings and also intersect with enduring discussions in the formal history of philosophy. Levi's analysis of these topics is at times original; where it is less so, it is nonetheless acute. That his discussion originates and accepts as a means of assessment the framework of historical aspects of the Holocaust provides continuity, in contrast to the variety of contexts that often give only disconnected items of historical evidence even where historical background is regarded as at all relevant. As physicians and engineers turn to stress tests to evaluate effects on the people or products they examine—at times, in engineering, testing those products "to destruction"—Levi examined moral and metaphysical ideas in the "laboratory" of Auschwitz and in the Nazi project more generally. The "laboratory" metaphor as applied to Auschwitz is one that he himself used; that he was part of the experiment did not deter him. The most obvious object of the stress test in Auschwitz was the Häftlinge; but ideas were also being put to the test, ideas whose histories over centuries had rarely come into view with the extremity or intensity contrived in Auschwitz. That someone who was himself being tested by these means should be capable at the same time of recognizing and reflecting on the practices makes Levi's work distinctive both as philosophy and as history and memoir.

The five topics considered here are the theories of human nature, evil (and good), justice and the "Gray Zone," the unspeakable, and God. I focus first on the ways Levi introduces them in his work and thought and then, necessarily more briefly, on their roles and configuration in the philosophical past.

THEORIES OF HUMAN NATURE

The concept of human nature, what humans are generically, has been a central concern of philosophy from Plato on, and recent discussions of that concept continue to crisscross the boundaries between philosophy and the social and natural sciences (the question's most concise version may remain that of Psalm 8: "What is man, that you remember him?"). The function of theories of human nature in cultural analysis is evident at both practical and theoretical levels: *any* account of what to expect or to require in human conduct necessarily draws on some such theory. So, for example, cultures or religions or governments rarely (arguably never) formulate laws or rules governing practices that have never occurred; thus, prohibitions appear as basic tell-tales of human conduct—what people *do*—and in this way they are also reports on what human nature is.

But however understandable the motivation impelling the question of what human nature is, it also encounters serious obstacles from its simplest origins. For in its basic formulation, what it seems to demand is a description of human nature "bare": unaffected by culture or history—in effect, outside time. Clearly, however, no such view of what persons essentially *are*— that is, a view from, and in effect of, nowhere—is possible on either theoretical or practical grounds. Newborn infants come immediately into specific environments, even then having left an obvious and important one behind; the most advanced technology has not yet found a means of directly inspecting Adam and Eve in the Garden of Eden. Yet an essentialist account of just this sort seems necessary if predictions or prescriptions concerning human conduct are to be proposed at all. It was to be expected, then, that in response to this pressure, various reconstructions should be attempted of human nature as it "really" is, and among this variety, two notably influential accounts provide both a background to and a sharp contrast with what then emerges as Primo Levi's critical response to them. All three of the accounts set out from the question of what can reasonably be inferred about essential human nature based on the evidence of how the people forced into the ghettoes and camps during the Holocaust reacted to those extreme circumstances. A dominant conclusion drawn from that evidence has been that the drive for individual survival which often led in those circumstances to the violation of standard ethical norms *also* revealed human nature as it truly was (indeed, revealed animal nature more generally): egoistic, competitive, aggressive.

To be sure, this view had had an influential history prior to the "test" case of the Nazi project, most notably in the reconstruction of a prehistorical "state of nature" allegedly inferred from the present condition of civil society (whenever that "present" was). The seventeenth-century English thinker Thomas Hobbes formulated a dramatic version of this reasoning in an account that seems on the surface commonsensical, even obvious. Look, Hobbes argues in *Leviathan*, at how people live in our own "civilized" world: locking their doors, walking about armed, hiring guards or police or armies—all these in order to prevent harm to themselves, their families, and their property. Imagine then the "state of nature" *without* such safeguards. And then we find Hobbes's hard-edged, concise description of life as it would be—according to him, as it had been—without any of the imposed constraints: "solitary, poor, nasty, brutish, and short," in what would surely have been a "war of every man against every man." All this, as Hobbes has it, because people in their natures are essentially individualist: competitive, self-seeking, prideful.

Hobbes then infers from this "original" state that the principal function of government is to provide security, enabling people as individuals to go about their business. Government's role is thus prophylactic, preventative—a conception of the role which thinkers following Hobbes developed more fully into the social contract theory of government that, with evolving adjustments and qualifications, remains a founding principle of liberal democracy according to which the role of government is only supplementary to the basic individual nature.

A parallel account of human nature has appeared recently that relies more directly on biology and genetics for uncovering the human "essence." In one of its versions, this account posits a dominant "selfish gene" which hardwires human nature as narcissistic: self-seeking and externally aggressive. Variations on this basic account turn to genetic combinations rather than to a single gene, or they find evidence for the same human characteristics in other members of the animal world that are then privileged as providing templates of human nature. In these variants, too, civil government and moral rules are no more than accommodations. Acts of altruism, for example, become aberrations or are reductively interpreted as further evidence for the centrality of self-interest, in which aggression is the response whenever self-interest is blocked. All these, again, rely on the assumption that egotism and individualism are essential and constant in human beings: what they are by *nature*.

Unsurprisingly, in these conceptions of human nature the descriptions of life in the ghettoes and camps during the Holocaust are interpreted as supporting evidence that points to the breakdown of conventional moral rules and the sense of ethical obligation not only among the perpetrators—more or less taken for granted—but among the victims themselves as they are increasingly pushed to extremity. Levi cites a fellow survivor from the Lager on what she had adopted as her own principle of survival: "First, I thought of myself; then I thought of myself also second; and then third, too." And in *If This Is a Man*, Levi himself recounts striking instances of this conduct from close range; for example, in the persona of Alfred L., who was so calculating in his self-regard that he managed to combine "maximum courtesy compatible with his egotism . . . [with the] cold life of the determined and joyless dominator." Or more spontaneously but no less extremely, in the dwarf Elias, who is "naturally and innocently a thief . . . [who] steals as fatally and foreseeably as a stone drops. . . . He has resisted annihilation from within because he is insane . . . the human type most suited to this way of living."[2] Elias does not *decide* to act in a particular way; he just *acts*. It thus comes as no surprise that behavior under the extreme conditions of the camps or ghettoes would be invoked in studies of human nature under other extreme situations, or that the same or related conclusions should be drawn. Well-known analyses of slavery in the United States and of the mechanism of authoritarian power in the Milgram and Zimbardo experiments have reached similar conclusions, as the violations of moral principle in the sources of authority and power become replicated on the part of the victims—thus arguing for a bedrock of human nature in self-regard and self-assertion.

But then comes Primo Levi, who lived through Auschwitz and is aware as he begins to write about the experience of the claims that the indifference to ethical norms in the camps revealed human nature as it really is. Levi, however, draws a radically different conclusion from the same evidence. Egoistic behavior in the camps, he argues, proves no more than that under *certain* conditions people tend to act in a certain way—with the clause "under certain conditions" crucial for understanding his reasoning. The key question Levi introduces here is why *that* behavior in *that* context should be judged more revealing of human nature than the fact that under other circumstances people conduct themselves quite differently. Since the judgment of "typical" human behavior in the camps is contextual (related to the extreme conditions there), any weight assigned it should apply only in comparison to *other* contexts. Viewed in these terms, it is a conceptual and in the end also a moral error to privilege one context over all others—and Levi objects to this sharply and emphatically: "We do not believe in the most obvious and facile deduction: that man is fundamentally brutal, egoistic and stupid in his conduct once every civilized institution is taken away, and that the Häftling is consequently nothing but a man without inhibitions. We believe, rather, that the only conclusion to be drawn is that in the face of driving necessity and physical disabilities many social habits and instincts are reduced to silence."[3]

Notice the authorial "we" Levi uses here, in contrast to his more common "I" and the occasional appearances of a collective but nonauthorial "we." His strenuous objection appears, furthermore, in the same text in which Levi also introduces a powerful counterexample to the theory of human nature he is criticizing, For he also shows that even under the Lager's extreme conditions, people were capable of acting on the basis of a common humanity—the principal and continuing example of which was the Italian non-Jewish laborer Lorenzo Perrone, who over a period of six months and at risk to himself contrived to provide a daily ration of soup for Levi which Levi credits with his survival.

What Levi articulates here is a contextual view of human nature in contrast to the essentialist views otherwise asserted: a situational view that differs from the others in emphasizing the *relationship* between human responses and the settings occasioning them. This shift does not mean that Levi does not recognize differences between humans and other animals. What he is objecting to in the leap from behavior in the Lager to a human essence is its assumption that conduct which is no more than skin-deep, suddenly and without explanation becomes defining. For Levi, skin-deep means just and only that. And here we may be hearing the voice of the industrial chemist who was an expert on enamel coatings for wires as he had become earlier for paints and varnishes—all of them, after all, types of skin (akin to eggshells, an extension of the analogy to which he also calls attention). His criticism, drawn from the Lager and directed against what is arguably the prevalent view of human nature, may appear at one level as only a methodological corrective. But given the many surveys of human nature that do not grasp or take seriously that corrective reasoning, the criticism is substantive, adding a significant consideration to understanding the question of what human nature "really" is.

EVIL (AND GOOD)

Evil, which came to be epitomized for Levi in actions of the Nazis, also became a puzzle for him—and so it remained. Odd as this may sound, the openly inconclusive (and as I shall suggest, inconsistent) conclusion of not being able to understand evil as it appears in the Nazi project represents an important advance in Levi's thinking, in effect a fruitful turn from the view that he set out from. Attuned to the "normal" premise of modern science that whatever is found in nature's stores is in principle intelligible—thus, nothing in experience is beyond interpretation or explanation—Levi was clearly an offspring of the Enlightenment, the "Age of Reason" which optimistically saw in human reason the capacity to portray and explain everything found in nature, human or other. On this principle, evil and wrongdoing should *also* be intelligible and open to explanation, and in many of their appearances Levi finds this to hold; so, for example, for food to be stolen under conditions of starvation is surely comprehensible—an explanation, whatever its status as a justification.

But what Levi saw at Auschwitz and in Nazi practices more generally were acts that did not qualify as utilitarian or based on any related explanation. He mentions, for example, that on the transport that took him to Auschwitz the aged and ill, including people close to death (some of whom did in fact die on the journey), were also forced onto the train. Since the purpose of transporting the "passengers" was to carry them to their deaths and since this group was already dying, what justification, he asks, could there be for this added suffering? Or again, in the Lager itself: with the death sentence fixed for all Jews brought to the camp, why torture or degrade them before implementing that sentence? Levi cites a number of relatively benign practices that also fall under this heading of "useless violence," ranging from the slogan at the entrance to Auschwitz (*Arbeit Macht Frei*, "Labor Makes [One] Free") to other slogans or regulations within the camp demanding personal cleanliness and the precise tailoring of uniforms (why should men's shirts be required to have exactly five buttons?) with no means provided of complying with them.

The strained justification for these instances of useless violence that was later proposed to his interviewer Gitta Serenyi by Franz Stangl, one-time commandant of Sobibor and Treblinka—that such measures were adopted in order to inure the camp guards to the harsher acts later to be required of them—did not satisfy Levi even in prospect: the network of practices that this explanation was to account for was too imaginative and intricate for Stangl's "modest" utilitarian goal. But this also meant, against Levi's commitment to the capacity of reason, that he could find *no* explanation for those practices—except, that is, for the choice of wrongdoing or evil initiated for its own sake, an option unintelligible for him since it seemed to go beyond reason itself. Because of this imponderable, he was at a number of points tempted by biological explanations for the Nazi project; for example, by Konrad Lorenz's hypothesis of innate group aggressiveness against other groups. At times he even turned to the extreme proposal of collective insanity as an explanation for the Nazis' plan of Jewish extermination, building here on his belief that the "Final Solution" could not have advanced as far as it did without the collaboration or at least concurrence of the larger part of the German populace, which must then also have been acting on something like a common motivation that was itself unintelligible.

In the end, however, Levi backs away from both those hypotheses—against the latter because of his reluctance to assign collective moral responsibility under any circumstance and against both of them because of their common assumption of biological determinism. Whatever the form of psychological or physical determinism in its diverse versions, Levi views that position as proving at once too much and too little: too much, as it undermines even the possibility of moral responsibility (how can wrongdoing be assigned when those "responsible" *could not have done* other than they did?); too little, as it fails to account for the distinctive fact that the Nazis, as he concluded, had first decided to do what they did and then did it. The recourse to insanity as an explanation is in any event a counsel of desperation, a confession of ignorance, of not *having* an explanation: if Levi was forced to admit the latter conclusion, as he finally was, he would do so without the obscuring lens of insanity.

Levi finds himself driven here to the position that wrongdoing as the Nazis imagined and practiced it may be actual and objective but nonetheless and even so unintelligible. The first part of this conclusion runs counter to the rationalist tradition—and it is in this reference especially that I cite the two conflicting claims in combination as an advance in Levi's thinking. In Plato and Spinoza, to name two major examples, evil is not actual, has no objective standing. It is viewed either as a privation of good with no positive quality of its own (for Plato), or as a matter of taste, of liking or disliking—a subjective response to occurrences that are in themselves value-neutral (for Spinoza). Levi thus finds himself caught between this rationalist tradition (his own in many other ways) and the harsh reality with which Nazi practice confronted him. At times he was himself accused of being soft, at least of being "forgiving" about the harsh facts of Nazi wrongdoing. But he explicitly rejected those charges (as brought, for example, by Jean Améry, for whom he otherwise had high regard). A penetrating example of Levi's insistence on this paradoxical sense of evil—the more noteworthy when compared to the many more heinous acts occurring at the same time—was one already mentioned, when the Kapo Alex, who finds his hands covered with oil "without hatred and without sneering . . . wipes his hand on my shoulder, both the back and the palm . . . to clean it."[4] On a much larger scale, Levi spoke out emphatically about the justice of the death penalties imposed at Nuremberg and later on the capital verdict passed on Adolf Eichmann, not only through his unforgiving poem "For Adolf Eichmann"—in which he wished for Eichmann not death but a "sleepless five million nights . . . visited every night by the suffering of everyone who saw"—but by his explicit affirmation of the verdict reached by the Israeli court. (It is relevant to note that even in relation to the Eichmann verdict, Levi was scrupulous to the point of feeling obliged to add that he did not know if he would himself have been able to carry out that death sentence—a consideration rarely raised even among those who most strongly favored the verdict.)

There was no doubt for Levi after his return from Auschwitz, then, about the force of evil as evil: its irreducibility. He had no illusions about the possibilities of overcoming that force; so he could write dispassionately if not with equanimity, soon after his one trip to the United States, that "the Good Samaritan ethic had no place in Auschwitz. Nor does it have much of a place in contemporary Manhattan."[5] But he also did not doubt that some judgments ascribing good or evil to human acts could be asserted with as much certainty and be no less grounded in evidence than any other judgments. Here he forthrightly overrode the common characterization of judgments involving ethics and values as less objective, less actual (if objective or actual at all) than assertions of matters of fact. These two basic claims—the intelligibility of nature, on one hand, and the objective existence of evil that was for him unintelligible, on the other—are incompatible, an unforgiving inconsistency. But Levi chose to accept and to live with the inconsistency rather than give up either of its two premises: nature *was* intelligible, and evil *was* real. It is an exemplary instance where accepting the grip of a contradiction rather than denying or evading it by repressing one of its components represents an intellectual advance.

JUSTICE AND THE "GRAY ZONE"

As Levi recognized an objective line between good and evil, he claimed that same status for an area between the two: neither black nor white but gray. In his assertion that this Gray Zone also has moral standing, it is important to note a number of features that he is *not* attributing to it. He is not reserving the zone for ethical judgments in which it is difficult to decide whether good or evil dominates. Of course he recognizes such occurrences, but they are not sufficient reason for assigning those instances to the Gray Zone; they are and remain hard cases. Nor does he admit to the Gray Zone the many examples in which an otherwise good person lapses, or in which a person responsible for repeated acts of wrongdoing does something "good." Such occurrences are common enough and warrant discussion—but, again, not as justifying a place in the Gray Zone. Nor is the Gray Zone meant to be a repository for "suspended" judgments—judgments that should not be asserted categorically because to do so would be to pass judgment through the superficiality of moral hindsight. The ease of such hindsight in contrast to the pressure of making difficult moral decisions in the present is obvious and constant—but this is in Levi's view no more reason for suspending moral judgments about the past than it is for never making moral judgments. The crucial issue for him is not whether those who pass the judgment first stood in the place of the person being judged but whether the evidence points one way or the other. He does not argue that such an act of empathy might not be relevant as an exercise, but that it does not imply a veto on judgment because of its own consequences. If standing in the place of the person being judged were accepted as a requirement, it would make many such judgments, *especially* those of extreme wrongdoing, impossible—and, indeed, this view is implicit in the fact that suspending judgment is never advocated for the great moral villains of history; we do not imagine having to "stand in the places" of Hitlers or Stalins before judging them.

Nor, finally and most fundamentally, is the Gray Zone a place to which *all* human beings—by the fact of human frailty—are granted access, since that would then enable them conveniently to respond to any moral charge with the indisputable claim that "I'm only human." Levi became especially sensitive to this interpretation in the post-Holocaust period as more details began to come out about both the "ordinariness" of the German perpetrators and the incidents of wrongful conduct among the victims in the camps and ghettoes. There were important things to be said on both sides of that issue in Levi's view, but he emphatically rejected any equation between the two—the homogenizing effect that would follow this broadening of the Gray Zone. So he speaks in his own voice from the center of his evidence: "I do not know . . . whether in my depths there lurks a murderer, but I do know that I was a guiltless victim and I was not a murderer. I know that the murderers existed . . . and that to confuse them with their victims is a moral disease."[6]

In contrast to these alternatives, the concept of the Gray Zone applies to morally charged conduct in a middle ground between good and evil, right and wrong, where neither side of those pairs covers the situation and where imposing one side or the other becomes itself for Levi a moral wrong. The leading example for the Gray Zone that Levi mentions in the chapter of *The Drowned and the Saved* with that phrase as its title concerns the men of the Sonderkommandos: Jews in the death camps assigned to work directly at and in the gas chambers—marshaling the victims, collecting and pillaging the corpses, conveying Jews to the crematoria. Members of the Sonderkommando knew what their work entailed; they also knew beforehand their own certain end, based on the fate of the Sonderkommandos before them. Nonetheless, in carrying out their work they gained a temporary reprieve from immediate selection and increased rations—incentives that might, if temporarily, preserve them at the line separating life from death. Distinguishing them even from Jewish Kapos, who gained power via their positions over others—something that Sonderkommando members did not do—Levi places them then in the Gray Zone where "good" is inapplicable because of the extreme quality of what they did and "evil" inapplicable because of the consequences facing them if they chose not to do it (an extreme choice, after all, that they did have). This does not mean that for Levi the actions of Sonderkommando members were justifiable or good—only that neither that category nor its opposite applies. The Gray Zone thus occupies its own autonomous domain: separate, yet still within the compass of ethical judgment.

Even on Levi's own conceptualization of the Gray Zone, there may be disagreement about which acts or people belong to it, and he was aware of that possibility. Flagrant wrongdoers, for example, might seek refuge in it as an alternative to the damning verdict of evil otherwise awaiting them; Levi pointed to just this phenomenon in the common defense by Nazi functionaries that they "were only following orders"—a claim which in Levi's opinion compounded rather than absolved their guilt. He proposes the S.S. man Muhsfeld, as a candidate for the Gray Zone just because he weighed the decision of whether a sixteen-year-old girl who had somehow survived the gas chamber should be allowed to live (and then decided that she should not). Levi decides that on balance Muhsfeld does not belong there and concurs in the verdict of the Polish court which in 1947 condemned him to death for the atrocities he had taken part in, but it is not clear why Levi would even consider the Gray Zone for Muhsfeld on the basis of the single possibly exceptional instance he cites. There are also other, arguably likelier candidates for the Gray Zone than the men of the Sonderkommando—for example, members of the Judenräte (Jewish Councils), many of whom found themselves not appointed by their communities but forced by the Nazis to accept the role, others of whom accepted the role in order to respond to the community's needs regarding food supplies, health measures, and so on. (Levi found himself agreeing in the main with Hannah Arendt's conception of the "banality of evil" as descriptive of Nazi functionaries, although he then dissented from her view of why, given her account, they could still be held accountable; he also did not agree with her charge against the Judenräte as in effect doing the Nazis' work for them— among the most contentious of the claims in her "report" on Eichmann.) Levi does discuss in relation to the Gray Zone the example of Chaim Rumkowski, "king" of the Lodz ghetto— but that as an example seems as idiosyncratic as Rumkowski himself, whose conduct hardly resolves or even poses the question of the status of Judenrat members as a group.

Most notable about the Gray Zone, this third modality of ethical judgment, is its delineation of an area that ethical theory has historically avoided: a category in addition to good and evil, right and wrong, that is nonetheless more than just a hard case of either or a mixture of the two (or a "holding area," like Limbo in Catholic doctrine except that external release may yet be granted there because of *subsequent* events). The reason why ethical theory had consistently stopped short of what Levi introduces here seems clear: the challenge of defining good and evil in their individual and "ideal" appearances is formidable—sufficiently difficult to make efforts that trim away at them appear trivial. Kant's Categorical Imperative— "Act in such a way that the maxim of your act would serve as a universal law"—exemplifies this absolutist character, with moral decisions and acts either meeting the Imperative's requirement or not. Among other objections, Kant's critics have argued that neither life nor ethics is as simple as he implies, and Levi is in effect agreeing with this. But he then goes farther in marking a place for judgments that are not bound to either of the two traditional categories but remain still within the bounds of ethics itself. The Gray Zone is in that sense beyond or at least outside good and evil but morally significant, at the boundary of those ethical judgments and yet warranting a place of its own within ethics. It is as objective and real as its two principal and more commonly recognized alternatives. This expansion is neither hairsplitting nor evasive, although both those charges have been raised against it. Quite the contrary, it is at once morally tough-minded and morally imaginative. For it assigns moral standing to a position that had been otherwise pushed aside in a way that denied any means of judging it in ethical terms and which is indeed no less categorical than the two more commonly recognized alternatives.

THE UNSPEAKABLE

The terms *unspeakable*, *ineffable*, *incomprehensible*, and *indescribable* are frequently used (often interchangeably) in reference to the Holocaust. The issue raised by these terms involves the relation between language and experience or, more generally, between language and history: are there intrinsic limits to the capacity of language to represent personal or collective experience? *All* experience? The most extreme moments or types of experience? A common feature of the terms cited in relation to the Holocaust (and elsewhere) is that they are intended figuratively rather than literally, meant to underscore the horrific character of the event. This figurative core clashes with the context in which each word is used: *indescribable* appears frequently in otherwise full and detailed descriptions. More rarely acknowledged when these terms appear is that not only are they figurative but that the figure of speech they embody— the aporia—surfaces in varieties of discourse and in accounts of experience that are not horrific at all, as, for example, in responses to the experience of beauty (*sublime, work of genius*) or moments of passion or love (*beyond words, divine*). An exemplary instance of this appears in *King Lear* when Lear challenges his daughter, Cordelia, to match her sisters' fervid expressions of love for him. But Cordelia instead chooses silence, telling her father that she does indeed love him but that unlike her sisters, she cannot "heave her heart into her mouth": the intensity of her feeling cannot find words; it remains unspoken because unspeakable.

There are evident differences among the terms mentioned—as between *indescribable* or *unspeakable*, for example, or *inexplicable* against either. Notwithstanding all his efforts, Levi felt that he had found no adequate explanation for the actions of the Nazis or of the Germans more generally. This did not mean that he thought those actions were inexplicable, that there could not be an explanation, only that he did not know what it was. This acknowledgment itself opens the possibility that language as a medium may itself never be fully or adequately representational of what it describes, and Levi, with all his powers of articulation, seemed constantly aware of that possibility. But insofar as that possibility holds at all, it would apply to the relation between language and experience or history as such and not uniquely to the relation between language and the events of the Holocaust. I have already noted Levi's own refusal to write about certain events or relationships, some of them of great importance for him (such as his group's execution of the two partisans and certain of his personal relationships). But those occasions for silence do not count as indescribable or inexplicable, since they mark personal boundaries that everyone draws between what they feel free to speak or write about and what they don't.

The basic principle for Levi on interpretation and explanation remained one that guided his work first as a student and then in his professions: whatever occurred in nature, including human history, is in principle intelligible and thus describable or "effable." Certain events or feelings may push closer than others to the limits of language, and Levi recognized that the Holocaust brought into view—more significant, brought into *existence*—certain practices or acts which the languages he knew had not anticipated or had words for. He also acknowledged that some accounts are more easily composed than others, but this does not point to anything intrinsically unspeakable; for him, the "limits of language" were indeed the "limits of the world." (The biblical Tetragrammaton itself, after all, was "speak*able*"—only forbidden *to be spoken* except by the high priest on the Day of Atonement.) Here, too, Levi retained the Enlightenment optimism and its continuing quarrel with obscurantism or mystification. Because of his personal reserve, which extended to professional matters as well, he rarely criticized other writers; the occasions when he does so are thus all the more notable. And he does so, as we have seen, with special force when he discusses writing about the Holocaust that mystifies it as "beyond words" or that turns the difficulty of the subject into obscure language or conceits. (The latter, again, figured in his criticism of Celan as a poet.) This fault in writing about the Holocaust is for him another form of exploitation: identifying what is describable as beyond that, but principally in the interests of evasion or false emphasis. The Holocaust is difficult to write about for Levi both because of its enormity and because of its personal reference for him—although it is for him also difficult *not* to write about for the same reasons. However commensurable or incommensurable with the Holocaust other historical atrocities had been or may yet be, moral enormity in human history even on a lesser scale would have posed similar difficulties of description. Levi understood what has in the post-Holocaust world become a commonplace: that the Nazi project not only invented a complex language of deception but, even deeper than that, set up practices and institutions for which the standard lexicons had not yet found words. Levi himself notes this in *If This Is a Man*, and at least some of that inadequacy has not changed. *Häftling*, for example, applies to a "prisoner," someone in custody; it hardly describes the status of those held in Auschwitz or any of the other death or concentration camps who were condemned to death at once determinate and indeterminate; *Ka-tzetnik* (from the letters *KZ* of *Konzentration*), although more precise than *Häftling*, has not gained currency, at least in part because it is nondescriptive. The list of such terms would include *Muselmann*, about which Levi writes rather loosely and even inaccurately; it includes the phrase "the Holocaust" itself, which Levi objected to and attempted to avoid, using *Lager* and *the camps* to stand in for the more general Nazi atrocities. *Genocide*, coined as concept and term by the jurist Raphael Lemkin late in World War II, became commonly applied only in the years following the war's conclusion. But that problem mirrors the relation between language and history more generally—the history of language as well as the history of history—even if it is especially pointed in the relation between language and the Holocaust.

Accounts that represent the historical event of the Holocaust as beyond words and then attempt to demonstrate this by writing about that event obscurely or by asserting the straightforward claim that it *is* beyond words seem to Levi equivalent to placing the Holocaust itself outside history: for Levi, a dangerous falsehood.

GOD

After a brief period of religious fervor at the time of his bar mitzvah, Levi, moved by what he then came to see as the straightforward power of scientific explanation, exemplified for one thing by Darwin on evolution, experienced a growing distance from religious doctrine and its quasi-historical status. Whatever doubts remained for him about God's nature or existence before his months in Auschwitz turned to certainty in the conclusion he reached about those questions during those months. That view is epitomized in an episode in *If This Is a Man* when, after a selection of Häftlinge to be sent to the gas chambers, Levi, who was among those passed over, sees "old

Kuhn praying aloud, with his beret on his head, swaying back-wards and forwards violently. Kuhn is thanking God because he has not been chosen. Kuhn is out of his senses. Does he not see Beppo the Greek in the bunk next to him . . . who is twenty years old and is going to the gas chamber the day after tomorrow . . . ? If I was God, I would spit at Kuhn's prayer."[7]

Elsewhere, Levi confronts more directly the claims of theo-dicy, the classic two-pronged affirmation of God's omnipotence and his beneficence as those became epitomized in G. W. Leib-niz's concise claim that this is "the best of all possible worlds." To that doctrine, common as it is not only to Judaism but to Western religions more generally, Levi objects as bluntly as the issue has ever been put: "There is Auschwitz, and so there can-not be God." His reasoning here has nothing subtle about it: what the Nazis did means either that God is not all-powerful or that he is not all-good (or both), implying that at least the God alleged to have *those* qualities does not exist. This conclu-sion seems so clear and self-evident to Levi that he does not bother to consider the numerous historical attempts that have been made to blunt or avoid it: the counterclaims that human understanding cannot grasp divine intentions, that what ap-pears on the limited surface of immediate experience as wrong-ful or injustice is ultimately made good in the larger and longer scheme of things, that evil occurs not by divine order but as humans abuse the power given them of free will (which itself then becomes a good justifying all consequences that follow from it), that occurrences like the atrocities of Auschwitz are not *violations* of faith and commitment but tests of them—and like any good tests, bound to be severe. Levi understood the difficulty for those who, unlike him, had stronger roots in the religiously observant Jewish tradition. He alludes to that dif-ficulty, for instance, in relation to Elie Wiesel's struggle with faith as he faced Auschwitz from a background of much stron-ger religious ties than Levi's. But so far as Jewish religious law and practice professed to speak in the name of divine authority, that claim must take its chances for Levi on the basis of human experience and reason: *his*. And those chances, he concluded from what he had seen and experienced, were not good: "If for no other reason than that an Auschwitz existed, no one in our age should speak of Providence."[8]

However severe and limited in its scope, there is nothing novel in the substance of Levi's objections here. Dostoyevsky had suggested that evidence against the claims of God's goodness and omnipotence was as compelling in the tears of a little child as in any of the much larger instances of human suffering: where the *quality* of evil is at issue, quantity is irrelevant. Furthermore, it is clear that Levi's strong feelings and harsh words about Kuhn are not refutations; he is not even arguing against the practice of "petitionary" prayer—the request to God to intervene in history in one's own favor or thanking him for having done so. His objection is to Kuhn's giving thanks in full knowledge that his survival at the time depended on the fact that others had been chosen for death, with the implication that this, too, was something to be thankful for.

Levi might be criticized here for considering only the literal meaning of religious prayer and practice, a mode of interpretation that in other contexts he himself often, even more typically, avoided. Certainly he does not consider certain standard alternative modes of interpreting religious texts; for one large example, understanding them not in their literal reference but as expressions of practice and tradition (that is, noncognitively), as many nonverbal practices or rituals are commonly rendered. He himself provides just such a version of *nonliteral* reading when he writes unexpectedly and admiringly about his reading of the *Shulchan Aruch* (Joseph Karo's sixteenth-century summary compilation of Jewish law): "I feel in this [book] a fascination which is for all time, the fascination of subtilitas, the disinterested game of the intellect . . . an ancient taste for bold decision, an intellectual flexibility that doesn't fear contradictions, indeed welcomes them as an inevitable ingredient of life, and life is Rule . . . order precisely over chaos."[9] High praise, to be sure, but notably given without commitment to the "rules" the *Shulchan Aruch* assembles, ranging from what may be carried (and how far) on the Sabbath to what determines the impurity of menstruation.

Levi's own continuing identification with the Jewish community seems to reflect this "noncognitive" commitment writ large. Since he gave Jewish religious doctrine no credence, his youthful self-identification as Jewish, which if anything strengthened in adulthood, would necessarily be cultural and social—and that connection seems to have been even stronger than Levi himself acknowledged. As noted earlier, his claim that his identity as a Jew was forced on him by others (meaning first the racial laws in Italy and then the Nazis) was only partly true. What he absorbed from his extended family when growing up in Turin shaped him in a way that resonated throughout his life and would have gripped him in his later life even without the racial laws and without Auschwitz. Here as in other instances, a person's understanding of his or her own identity can be assessed and in the event disputed by others who view that sense of identity from the outside. And then, too, it has to be recognized that Levi's skepticism about what was taken to be orthodox doctrine and practice is far from exceptional in modern expressions of the Jewish tradition, as secular Judaism has claimed a growing place in the community. Even that, to be sure, had precedents on which to build and of which Levi was well aware; it is surely no accident that the first entry in Levi's personal anthology of literary works that influenced him in *The Search for Roots* was a selection from the biblical book of the contentious—and skeptical—Job. That Job finally was silent in contrast to Levi seems less relevant than the impulse for questioning itself.

What importance, then, should be ascribed to the concept of God in Levi's thinking and writing? In one sense, his position on that concept, unlike that on the other four issues discussed here, takes up no more space in his writing and thinking than it does in that of many other skeptics for whom the verdict on the concept is so clear as to require little in the way of disputation. When he responds to the question of what his religion is, he forthrightly says, "I have no religion," and in a similar context, "I am a nonbeliever." How much more than that, after all, would need to be filled in? But to understand Levi's search within other fields and his grasp of them, the unified network of his reasoned discourse, his continuous critique of obscurantism and his overriding moral concern are to recognize that not only are those commitments compatible with such skepticism but that they gain impetus from it—not as their only possible source but as an actual one. It would be a distortion here to ascribe to Levi Voltaire's view that "If God did not exist, it would be necessary to invent him"; for Levi, God's nonexistence, even in the radical, in some ways reductive, conception of the God whom he rejects, spreads throughout his thinking in the form of positive affirmation as well. This is not to say that any commitment as passionate and sustained as Levi's *amounts to* the assertion of a unifying cause—for example, to a basis analogous to William James's assertion in a different context of recognizing a "moral equivalent of war," which might here be viewed in Levi's commitment to a moral (and reasoned) equivalent of God. Levi's thinking is not immune to inconsistency and to other specific challenges in the large expanse it covered. But in the connectives between his thought and his writing we see at least an attempt to account for these lacunae. Readers of Levi have often found it easy to forget the claim he repeatedly made that he considered himself an optimist—notwithstanding his recognition and harsh descriptions of atrocity, violence, and malevolence. Certainly

he exceeds Antonio Gramsci's telling psychological characterization of "pessimism of the intellect, optimism of the will":
for Levi, there was optimism of the intellect no less than of the
will. Would there not be a presumed and conceptual source for
that claim? And even the end he put to his life does not detract
from the force of that combination.

These forays into Levi's thinking or even "philosophy" do
not argue for or against his views, although what I take to be the
validity of some of what he affirms may be evident, along with
certain difficulties about other parts. But however one judges
his individual views, the importance should be clear of recognizing the close connection between those sometimes abstract
analyses and the concrete historical detail on which he bases
them. Some of the positions attributed here to Levi have more
complex histories than have been discussed (such as theodicy,
divine providence, and the concept of God more generally).
Others, like the Gray Zone, stand at the beginning of what
would warrant a fuller account, and theories of human nature
continue to be debated in neuroscience and the social sciences
as well as in philosophy. Levi, as he has been presented, might
find many critics as well as allies on some or even most of these
issues among philosophers, fellow scientists, and writers.

But the dominant impress of Levi's ideas remains the link
between his thinking and the historical framework from which
it emerged and by which he tested his conclusions. Even in
his many writings that had nothing to do with the Holocaust,
he took history seriously—a quality often wanting in philosophical analysis, as it is often absent also in the social sciences.
Admittedly, to take history seriously is no guarantee of philosophical depth or insight, but it is arguably a condition for
seeing through and to the bottom of many, arguably all philosophical questions. When one adds to this feature of Levi's
writing his *compassion* for what he sees in history, his writing

becomes still more distinctive. In addition to his reference to Auschwitz as a laboratory, Levi at another point refers to it as having been a "university" for him. Somehow, even with his life in peril, he maintained a distance of observation, almost of experimentation, between himself and his surroundings. Of course, that extraordinary "university" was forced on him; nobody would advocate it as a forum of education. But Levi responds to the challenge by taking experience and history both as conditions that set the stage for thinking and then as incentives for *doing* that thinking. What he then accomplished was to link the practice of writing with idea and principle as cogently as anyone who has written about the Holocaust. This connection would warrant recognition of his ideas as important whether identified as philosophical or not; it extended in some of his writings to work that has sometimes been called "science fiction"—a genre necessarily grounded in *nonfiction* for credibility. The concepts and ideas about which he reflects and argues consistently remain integral to the experience in which they originate; this itself remains a bequest to his readers also in their experience and thinking.

6

The Beginning

THE BEGINNING? Asserted, one supposes, with the force of
the Hebrew Bible at *its* beginning: "In the beginning . . ." When
attached to *beginning*, *the*—that slight but definite article—
implies that there was only the one beginning for that particular event: nothing came before or even alongside it. So: Primo
Michele Levi was born in Turin on July 31, 1919. Was *that* the
beginning? Well yes—but also no. Yes, because on July 30, he
was not Primo Levi, and then on July 31 he was. Sort of. Some-
where in that interval, there certainly was "a" beginning, but
not necessarily or even probably "the" beginning. For mixed
in the interval were also the months of gestation before July
30—surely they would have their say, as would also his parents
(Cesare and Ester), from whose own genes, patrimonies, and
heritages Primo drew not only at his birth but in all his future
years when he was becoming and then became Primo Levi.
Those ingredients would rise to the surface sequentially, like

time capsules: genes, family links, social class, language(s), received wisdom, taboos. There is no way to filter or reduce this ocean of factors. The attempt could be made, and has been on a much larger scale, to narrow the causes at the moment that Primo Levi became the person he was—for example, to admit only biology or genetics. But even then "the" beginning would be expansive, extending back to ancestors and great-ancestors and great-great-ancestors, eventually arriving at a version of Adam and/or Eve so remote from the chain of questions that began much more simply in asking when did Primo Levi became Primo Levi; that is, when did *that* beginning—his—occur.

The book of Genesis had indeed offered a convenient refuge when it circumvented biology. But theology also relies on assumptions, most immediately that there *must* have been not only "a" beginning, but "the" one and only. This assumption becomes flagrant if one only reaches across from the Hebrew to the Greek world, where there was little anxiety about *the* beginnings of anything, with the effects of that absence prominent in Greek culture and practice. As, for example, in the Greeks' avoidance of the idea of progress that involves not only movement from one historical phase to another but a point-by-point improvement on the past that is then incorporated into future points. Imagine then, contrarily, "the beginning" as an artifice or conceit, a means of introducing not the *history* of an event or person but the *narrative* about it, much like the function of "Once upon a time," which provides entree to stories that we now take for granted as a figment of the story rather than of the events that may or may not have happened once—or even twice—upon a time.

The Greeks brought to light numerous cosmologies and no doubt a variety of other expressions of anxiety but not any about "the" beginnings. Their version of "starting points" inclined rather to the alternative of cycles or circles, even repetition, of the past for which starting points would not be true beginnings but momentary resting points: history as recurrence, not as linear. And this would mandate a flat denial of creation from nothing, as in the Big Bang theory, with its divine or subatomic or sexual overtures. Aristotle considered the theory of creation from nothing a fifth wheel, a needless assumption—and even the pious Maimonides found his objection plausible before moving on to the both plausible and biblical account of "the" beginning. So think rather of circles than of lines—with the circles or cycles perhaps large and long (ten thousand years in the Stoics' version), but with the exact length a much lesser matter than the benefit of dispelling the concern about a beginning. For with beginnings, it should also be remembered, comes anxiety also about "the end"—since the mind continues to travel on the same track on which the beginning begins, moving on then to balance it with a correspondingly unique end. Thus the array extending from messianism to apocalypse, an expanse of possibilities of which many have then surfaced as actual.

Still, cosmology is not biography, and the question of when Primo Levi became Primo Levi does not go away. Would it have been when, at age thirteen, he formally "became" a man, in the passage of becoming bar mitzvah? Or with the advance of another decade, as he rose to become *Doctor* Levi, with the honors of his university degree and soon afterward in the identity of a working chemist? But the marker would be placed still more dramatically in his months as a partisan and then in Auschwitz; no other events had greater individual force, before or after. On the other hand (the fourth or fifth), the claim might also apply to the moment when he found himself freed from Auschwitz and an unexpected survivor—when, still dizzied by that realization, he was overwhelmed by the impulse to describe what he had undergone and seen. But then, too, in the lengthy (forty-year) aftermath of that liberation—together with marriage and becoming a parent—he began to think of himself as being a writer as well as a chemist, eventually *more* a writer than a chemist; that development, too, would have a firm grip on Levi's becoming Levi. Although perhaps no more than the lasting occurrence of the question of whether it was "the" Primo Levi who, on April 11, 1987, in the same building in which he had been born (*that* beginning), committed suicide. Many who agree with that verdict and still more those who continue to dispute it would argue that whatever happened on that morning at Corso Re Umberto 75, Primo Levi at the time was "not himself" (although if not himself, then who?). And in fact, the unfolding does not end even there, since Levi's afterlife must also be considered: his afterlife in *this* world. For that has continued not only to grow but to evolve, at times proposing to recast his life as a whole and continuing to do this now as well, twenty-five years after his biological death. There is no reason to think that the continuation of his life in this way will end at any time soon. So Primo Levi seems still to be becoming Primo Levi.

Here again, however, a conceptual question interrupts. For to ask when Primo Levi became Primo Levi presupposes that there was and should be only *one* Primo Levi, an essence or core that he would and did become, a unified self encompassing and overriding the diverse, at times conflicting moments and expressions in his history. Perhaps there are indeed life-trajectories unified in this way, pointed, at least in retrospect, in a single direction—as if a goal had been set initially, a "final cause," with which history, for all its apparent accidents, fell into a straight line. Or in a milder version, an evolving principle or axis (still a single one) that might seem to change course at times but in the end found continuity also in those changes. The life and the person would in this way indeed have an essence or center, perhaps unknown even to the individual but evident from the outside. As so much else can be known about a person from the outside that is unknown or less known to the person from within (starting, as Levi himself suggested, with one's face, which is much more familiar to others than to the self whose face it is). Such a center or axis would indeed make an intelligible whole out of what otherwise would seem only fragments, at most a pastiche.

This account of unity is plausible, but it may also gain its persuasiveness as the sort of story we like to tell ourselves. For on inspection of actual persons and their histories—which often include earthshaking events among others much less so—such unity seems improbable, certainly rare. And Primo Levi is a good example here, for notwithstanding the several dramatically overpowering events in his life, it is clear that smaller, less obtrusive ones also had significant roles. To reach the conclusion of a single trajectory or essence to his person—*the* Primo Levi—decisions would have to be assumed and made not only about exactly which events set the direction of the trajectory, but also about those that for whatever reasons did not. The issue here resembles—in a way is identical to—the problem facing the doctrine of the resurrection of the dead: at exactly what age in their lives would the dead be resurrected? To claim the same age for everybody seems arbitrary (especially for those who died in infancy)—and then too, whatever the age, the decision would be assumed on why the specific age(s) cited should have precedence over others.

In this fog of doubts, furthermore, there remains also the matter of counterfactual history: What would Levi have become if such and such which did not happen had happened—or if such and such which did happen had not happened. Those questions came his way repeatedly, and one in particular epitomizes the issue: the matter of whether he would have become a writer if not for Auschwitz. Counterfactual—for he was a Häftling in Auschwitz (number 174517) and he became a writer soon after being freed, and nobody doubts that those two "moments" were connected. Of course the safest response to the counterfactual question must be that it is impossible to know what would have come of Levi without the interruption of what had before that been an orderly and predictable life. Levi himself responded with this caution often—but not always, since he suggested at other times both that he would not have become a writer if not for Auschwitz and that he might well have become a writer anyway. But the question edges into a larger sphere than only that of Levi's profession, since it impels the broader question of whether the Auschwitz months were or were not the central core around which Levi's life afterward revolved and evolved, responsible for everything that followed, including his becoming a writer and the sort of writer he became and the many other parts of his life, even his death. His turn to writing would thus have been a key—*the* key—to understanding the broad expanse of his rich life in the forty years after Auschwitz.

The impact of the Auschwitz months on Primo Levi cannot be doubted, and nobody does. His earliest books, the first published in 1947, the second in 1963, differed in register and genre, but the hard fact of Auschwitz moved them both. Had Levi stopped writing after the second book, there would be no alternative to agreeing on the centrality of Auschwitz for his writing—and to understanding his writing as tied entirely to that experience, even if the writing in the books themselves might suggest otherwise. What he would have been doing instead during the period after *The Truce* appeared, presumably with the same energy in other enterprises that was so distinctive a feature of Primo Levi, is an intriguing question, though even more than other counterfactuals a difficult one to find a way through. To be sure, a portentous moment in 1963 bears on the question: when asked in an interview with Pier Maria Paoletti soon after he received the Campiello Prize for *The Truce* whether he planned to continue writing about the Lager and the Germans, he responded swiftly and categorically: "Absolutely not another word. Nothing. I've said everything I have to say."[1] The questioner admittedly did not ask whether Levi would continue *writing*, only whether he would continue writing about what had been then his principal subject; the unequivocal answer he gave to that was soon proven to be mistaken—not about the role of author but about the author's subjects.

Of course, nobody would hold Levi to account for this prediction that he himself would disprove; he obviously did reverse himself, emphatically, in, among other works, the novel *If Not Now, When?* (1984) and his last book, *The Drowned and the Saved* (1986). What that response does foreshadow, however, is his regard for writing even then as pointed in directions in addition to and other than the German (or the Jewish) Question. And indeed diversity of several kinds—subjects, genres, timbres—not only characterizes his subsequent career as writer, but in that it reflects also back on the two early books about the Holocaust—demonstrating, if their readers had missed it, that although subject and form in those books were surely related, Levi's power as a writer went beyond their particular subject, irrespective of how momentous it was—it would, and should, place him in a tradition of writers most of whom had lived and written long before Auschwitz cast its shadow. If the Lager triggered the impulse of writing in him, to claim that his capacity for doing this was *created* then goes beyond the evidence and against some of it. Levi himself did not know when or how that impulse or the capacity to realize it "began"; there is no reason to think that he ever discovered it or the origins of his many other sides, and it is no easier to answer these questions now from the outside than it would have been for him from the inside.

All these surmises or quibbles suggest that the questions may themselves be beside the point, at least beside any point that would reveal "the" Levi at the center of the often disso-

Levi's grave, Jewish communal cemetary.

nant assembly of the pushes and pulls impelling his individual decisions as they together, his Collected Works in a more than only literary sense, represent him. As one reads and thinks about Primo Levi, it becomes increasingly clear that the whole of him is more than the sum of its parts. That may be true to an extent for all people, perhaps linked to the distinguishing features of an individual person. But the realization of this truth about Primo Levi comes more quickly and decisively than it does for many others; that realization might also be understood as the beginning of an end, of his biography if not of his life.

PREFACE

Attempting to describe how I came to write a book about Primo Levi's life and thought would shift from his biography to my own autobiography, and although the latter is the more malleable form—its checkpoints internal against the biographer's primary obligation to the external evidence—the result would be diversionary, of less interest to Levi's readers and even to myself. But this same reservation points to my principal incentive for undertaking the book and then staying with it: a conviction which grew with my writing of Levi's extraordinary grasp of the human moral condition and of the imagination that motivated (often enough, to deplore) it, joined then with his ability to provide access to those findings—*pleasurable* access—even when what he was writing about was horrific and painful.

One source of Levi's reach in these directions was his rejection of the alleged divide between "two cultures," science and the humanities, that C. P. Snow's formulation made a topic of discussion during Levi's most creative period. Levi himself was dismayed that anybody would regard that divide as credible: centuries earlier, he reminded an interlocutor, Galileo had shown how little the alleged division mattered. Nor does the fluent range of Levi's writing simply reflect his combination of a respected, even distinguished career in industrial chemistry and his extraordinary literary achievements. Underlying all these expressions is the power of a mind that understood nature, human and other, as unified and intelligible, with all its parts inviting, even demanding reflection, commentary, invention: the common grain of sand that would nourish varieties of pearl. The effect here, needless to say, goes beyond the "interdisciplinary." Levi attached little significance to the institutional disciplines, which in his view had much more in common than they had separating them, even granting the specialization they might individually require. Unapologetically and without denying or obscuring the differences in their moral consequence, his demanding curiosity would find its way to subjects as disparate as Auschwitz and the remarkable jumping ability of fleas compared to that of human beings. Levi observed the world through a lens for which nothing was alien— not only nothing *human*, but nothing.

Such comments are not meant to claim a place for Levi among the canonical "greats"—literary, philosophical, or scientific. Figures like Shakespeare, Plato, and Darwin have continuously succeeded in reestablishing themselves, typically growing larger over time than they were in their initial reception, in part because of their cumulative momentum but also because of what they were in themselves. But the manner of their achievements differed, and in that respect, too, Levi may be found among them. Among the factors contributing to his accomplishments is one often seen as secondary but which I have attempted to present as primary. Levi's earliest readers came to him through his account of the eleven months of his captivity in Auschwitz (*If This Is a Man*, 1947) and, sixteen years later, his account in *The Truce* of his protracted, nine-month return to Turin after being liberated. The focus in the first book was on the Lager and the Nazi system of extermination; in the second that experience, although still in the background, was still dominant. Readers drawn to these books typically regarded them first as reflections of a survivor and only second, if at all, as literary achievements. Levi himself explicitly denied literary intentions in the first of these, and that is clearly the way that his early readers by and large received it.

But authorial claims of intention have limited authority over interpretations of the work, and although the importance of Auschwitz did not diminish for Levi after the publication of those books, he also began to write intensely about other subjects in a way that encouraged reflection on the literary features of the earlier books as well. Some of his later works, like *The Periodic Table*, mingled references to the Lager with other subjects; others made no reference to that experience. In Levi's remarkably productive period of almost twenty-five years after *The Truce* was published (almost half that time preceded his retirement from the chemical factory, when writing became his sole "full-time" profession), much the larger part of his oeuvre appeared. And there the range of subjects to which he turned reflected the wide range of his curiosity: nature's own ironic disposition and the scientific intrigue in human efforts to decipher and understand it; the importance for human self-realization of labor, the job of work, and the skills required for it (which brought him into unusual conflict with Italy's political left); the craft of writing itself as the writer conceived and practiced it; the range of human emotions more generally—love, friendship, anger, regret. He expressed these, moreover, in a variety of genres: fictions short and long, essays, poetry. In this respect, too, Levi regarded the conventional boundaries of expression always as negotiable, as if inviting crossover.

It was not that during these later years Levi moved away in his concern and thinking from the Nazi atrocities; his last and for many readers his most important book during his final years—*The Drowned* (literally, "Submerged") *and the Saved*—focused entirely on the Lager. But he repeatedly also denied then, as he often had earlier in the forty years after his return from captivity to Turin, that the Lager was the primary or even more certainly the exclusive factor in shaping his life, his writing, or his thinking. He increasingly thought of himself as a writer who confronted the Holocaust as an element in his writing—*not* as a Holocaust writer who had an interest in other topics as well. The evidence of his writing itself supports this self-assessment, as it also sets him apart from many other writers, however accomplished, for whom the Holocaust has remained at once an exclusive and an exclusionary subject. To place Levi in this group would be to confront the difficulty of explaining Levi's repeated insistence that notwithstanding the darkness he often portrayed—and his own private darkness into which he periodically fell—he considered himself basically an optimist. And that in his calling as a writer, the author he would choose as his literary father, to whom he "felt closest, almost like a son," was Rabelais. (In lectures, I've asked audiences what author they thought he would be likely to have chosen in this paternal role; Rabelais has *never* been among the candidates proposed.)

This expansion of the narrower framework in which the figure of Levi as author is more often set does not deny (how could it?) his constant reference to his own Jewish identity and the historical framework of twentieth-century Europe in which Jews played such a prominent, if often involuntary, part. (His awareness of history as he wrote about his often nonhistorical interests constantly reinforces his distinctiveness as a writer.) And this combination also emphasized for me the challenge of finding a place for Levi in the Yale University Press series of biographies published under the rubric of "Jewish Lives." That Levi *was* Jewish, neither he nor others around him—enemies or friends—ever doubted. But the series title "Jewish Lives" seemed to suggest that that rubric was self-explanatory, and this is clearly not the case. Does it refer to one of the measures of genetic lineage? To upbringing? Cultural memory or affiliation? Persecution? Many *types* of "Jewish lives" have surfaced in the three thousand years of Jewish history, with many among those types sharply opposed to the inclusion of others: these, too—candidates and excluders both—remain part of the variety. Levi himself, whatever else he might say about *this* biography—a prospect I would at once fear and cherish—would probably not quarrel with its inclusion in a series titled "Jewish Lives," although he might also hope that other versions of his biography would appear in series with titles pointed in other directions: "Literary Lives," "Twentieth-Century Lives," "Piedmont Lives." I would certainly understand that wish, although I might hope that this "life" would have a chance of appearing even (or also) among them.

* * *

My daughter, Ariella Lang, was a partner in the search and research for this book; I have depended on her judgment and resourcefulness, her grasp of Italian culture and history, and her ability to bring these to bear on Primo Levi's life and times. Steven Zipperstein and Anita Shapira, coeditors of the Yale University Press series Jewish Lives, have lent supportive confidence to the book as a project; they have also awaited it with unusual patience. Longer acquaintance with Steven as scholar and editor has led to more frequent discussions with him and thus also to my sense of a special debt. Murray Baumgarten, Robert S. C. Gordon, Nancy Harrowitz, Vivian Mann, Howard Needler, and Hayden White have in a variety of readings and listenings drawn my attention to aspects of Primo Levi's life that I would otherwise have missed. John Palmer and Susan Laity of Yale University Press have been both generous and expert in seeing the book through the editorial process.

Anybody who writes about Primo Levi must appreciate the biographical and critical material concerning Levi that has been gathered in the constantly growing Levi literature; in this sense Levi himself has become a center of devoted attention. I would mention here especially work from which I have drawn by Carole Angier, Myriam Anissimov, Marco Belpoliti, Robert S. C. Gordon, and Ian Thomson. Different as these authors' approaches and often conclusions are in voice and texture, their shared commitment to Levi's thought and writing is as extraordinary as it is exemplary—though not, as his readers would quickly recognize, surprising; few contemporary or near-contemporary writers have won the intense and sustained admiration that Levi has.

I am grateful to colleagues and students in the College of Letters and the Department of Philosophy at Wesleyan University, where I was teaching while engaged in much of the work on this book; also to audiences at Wesleyan, the Hebrew University, Ben Gurion University, Indiana University, and the University of Chicago who responded to lectures or discussions I engaged in there. The Yad Vashem Center for Holocaust Studies in Jerusalem provided a Research Fellowship in the spring of 2012 that enabled me to "sit" at the Center and make use of its facilities for that time, with gratifying opportunities for discussion and collegiality.

Barbara Estrin, to whom I dedicate the book, contributed to its substance and structure from its beginning (indeed, from before its beginning) in more ways than I can describe. A writer could hope for no more than that her caring intelligence and her acute sensibility for language and issues would be evident in the text itself.

With such generous support, it becomes a greater obligation still to acknowledge that mistakes and misjudgments remaining in the book are, alas, my own.

CHRONOLOGY

1918	October 7: Marriage of Cesare Levi, electrical engineer (b. 1878), and Ester Luzzati (b. 1895). The two reside thereafter at Corso Re Umberto 75, Turin.
1919	July 31: Birth of Primo Michele Levi (P.L.).
1921	January 21: Birth of P.L.'s sister, Anna Maria Levi.
1922	October 28: March on Rome brings Mussolini and the Fascist Party to power.
1934–37	P.L. enrolled at Liceo Massimo d'Azeglio.
1937–41	P.L. enrolled at the University of Turin, graduating with highest honors in chemistry.
1938	September 6: First anti-Jewish legislation promulgated in Italy.
1942	P.L. finds work as chemist in Milan. March 24: Death of P.L.'s father, Cesare.

1943	September 8: Italian armistice with Allies; Mussolini deposed.
	October 1: P.L. joins partisan group in Piedmont.
	December 12–13: P.L. and other members of group captured by Italian Fascist Militia.
1944	January 27: P.L. transferred to holding camp at Fossoli.
	February 22: Transport begins for 650 Italian Jews, including P.L., to Auschwitz.
	February 26: Transport reaches Auschwitz; P.L. tattooed as 174517.
1945	January 27: Russian army liberates Auschwitz; P.L. in camp infirmary.
	March 6: P.L. is moved to a Russian assembly camp at Katowice, Poland; he remains there four months and two additional months in an assembly camp at Starya Dorogi, in the Soviet Union.
	September 15: P.L. sets out for Italy by train.
	October 19: P.L. reaches Corso Re Umberto 75.
1946	January 21: P.L. begins work as chemist at Duco Avigliana.
1947	Manuscript of *If This Is a Man* is submitted to Einaudi and rejected.
	September 8: P.L. marries Lucia Morpurgo in civil and Jewish ceremonies.
	October 11: *If This Is a Man* is published in Turin by De Silva Press.
1948	P.L. begins work as chemist at Società industriale vernici e affini (SIVA), where he will work until 1974.
	October 31: Birth of daughter, Lisa.
1952	Einaudi rejects P.L.'s proposal to publish new edition of *If This Is a Man*.

1955	Einaudi agrees to P.L.'s new proposal to publish new edition of *If This Is a Man;* publication is delayed until 1958.
1957	July 2: Birth of son, Renzo.
1963	*The Truce* is awarded the first Campiello Prize for literary distinction; the prize is after that awarded annually.
1968	March 17: Beginning of week-long trip to Israel.
1974	P.L. retires from SIVA.
1985	April 12: Beginning of three-week visit to the United States.
1986	Publication of *The Drowned and the Saved.*
1987	April 11: P.L. dies at Corso Re Umberto 75.

BOOKS BY PRIMO LEVI

The two-volume edition of Levi's works (*Opere*) edited by Marco Belpoliti was published by Einaudi in 1997.

Black Hole of Auschwitz, The. Trans. Sharon Wood. Ed. Marco Belpoliti. Cambridge: Polity, 2005. *Asimmetria e la vita: articoli e saggi, 1955–1987*. Turin: Einaudi, 2002.

Collected Poems. Trans. Ruth Feldman and Brian Swann. London: Faber and Faber, 1988. *Ad ora incerta*. Milan: Garzanti, 1984.

Drowned and the Saved, The. Trans. Raymond Rosenthal. London: Michael Joseph, 1988; New York: Vintage, 1989. *I sommersi e salvati*. Turin: Einaudi, 1986. [*Sommersi* literally means "submerged," *not* "drowned"; this difference is captured in the German (der Untergegangenen) and the French (les naufrages) titles.]

If Not Now, When? Trans. William Weaver. London: Michael Joseph, 1986; New York: Summit, 1986. *Se non ora, quando?* Turin: Einaudi, 1984.

If This Is a Man. Trans. Stuart Woolf. London: Orion, 1959; sub-

159

PRIMO LEVI

sequently retitled *Survival in Auschwitz*. New York: Collier, 1993. *Se questo è un uomo*. Turin: De Silva, 1947 (reissued by Einaudi in 1958).

Mirror Maker, The. Trans. Raymond Rosenthal. London: Methuen, 1990; New York: Schocken, 1989. Selections from *Racconti e saggi*. Turin: La Stampa, 1986.

Moments of Reprieve. Trans. Ruth Feldman. New York: Summit, 1986. Condensed from *Lilìt e altri racconti*. Turin: Einaudi, 1978.

Other People's Trades. Trans. Raymond Rosenthal. London: Michael Joseph, 1986; New York: Summit, 1989. *L'altrui mestiere*. Turin: Einaudi, 1985.

Periodic Table, The. Trans. Raymond Rosenthal. London: Michael Joseph, 1975; New York: Schocken, 1984. *Il sistema periodica*. Turin: Einaudi, 1975.

Search for Roots, The: A Personal Anthology. Trans. Peter Forbes. London: Penguin, 2001; Chicago: Ivan R. Dee, 2002. *La ricerca delle radici*. Turin: Einaudi, 1981.

Shema: Collected Poems. Trans. Ruth Feldman and Brian Swann. London: Menard, 1976. *L'osteria di Brema*. Milan: Scheiwiller, 1975.

Sixth Day, The. Trans. Raymond Rosenthal. London: Michael Joseph, 1990; New York: Summit, 1990. Selections from *Storie naturali*. Turin: Einaudi, 1966, and *Vizio di forma*. Turin: Einaudi, 1971.

Truce, The. Trans. Stuart Woolf. London: Bodley Head, 1965; *The Reawakening*. New York: Macmillan, 1986. *La tregua*. Turin: Einaudi, 1963.

Wrench, The. Trans. William Weaver. London: Michael Joseph, 1987; *The Monkey's Wrench*, New York: Summit, 1987. *La chiave a stella*. Turin: Einaudi, 1978.

NOTES

All citations from Primo Levi's *If This Is a Man* are to the American edition, retitled *Survival in Auschwitz*.

Chapter 1. The End

1. Quoted in Ian Thomson, *Primo Levi: A Life* (New York: Picador, 2002), p. 519. Levi, in parts of his unpublished correspondence with Hety Schmitt-Maas (November 2–8, 1967), details some of the sources of this resentment, and although these are expressed *after* twenty years of marriage, they reflect what earlier evidence has indicated as well.

2. Quoted in Thomson, *Primo Levi*, p. 526.

3. This absence has sometimes been regarded as counterevidence to the verdict of suicide, although studies have invariably noted this phenomenon in a majority of cases: notes are left, according to one study, in only one of six suicides. See Michael Graham Geller, Richard Mayon, and John Geddes, *Psychiatry* (New York: Oxford University Press, 2005).

4. Quoted in *La Stampa*, April 14, 1987. Levi notes also that he had no memory of Jean Améry, who claimed that he and Levi had been in the same hut in Monowitz for several weeks; Levi did not rule out the possibility, although he also makes the statement "I preserve of Auschwitz a total, indelible memory" (*The Drowned and the Saved*, p. 130).

5. One such judgment from small-town Connecticut in the 1940s exemplifies this. A local Jewish man drowned in a river that ran through the town; with no evidence that the man had not gone voluntarily into the river, the coroner's verdict was suicide. The community rabbi ruled, however, that even on the assumption that the man deliberately went into the river, it was impossible to know without the evidence of eyewitnesses (of which there were none) whether he did not *then* attempt to return to shore. In the absence of that evidence, Rabbi Rosenberg held, the verdict of suicide must be withheld.

6. Levi, *The Drowned and the Saved*, p. 159.

7. See Jean Améry, *On Suicide: A Discourse on Voluntary Death*, trans. John D. Barlow (Bloomington: Indiana University Press, 1999). Originally published as *Hand an sich Legen* (Stuttgart: Klett-Cotta, 1976). In a letter to Hety Schmitt-Maas after Améry's suicide (October 17, 1978), Levi wrote, "Suicides are generally mysterious: Améry's was not." So Améry would write in *At the Mind's Limits*, not long before his suicide: "Twenty two years later, I am still dangling over the ground by dislocated arms" (trans. Sidney Rosenfeld and Stella P. Rosenfeld [Bloomington: Indiana University Press, 1980], p. 36). Later, after the suicide of his friend Hanns Engert, Levi wrote, "Suicide is a right we all have" (cited in Thomson, *Primo Levi*, p. 423).

8. In an interview (January 17, 1983) with Anna Bravo and Federico Cereja, Levi claimed about this: "There were very few suicides in the Lager. . . . My interpretation is that suicide is a human act, since animals don't commit suicide, and the human tended towards the level of the animal in the camps, so that . . . it was the business of the day that matters. . . . There was no time to think about killing yourself." But then, in response to the com-

ment "But it must have been one way of putting an end to the suffering," Levi admitted, "I thought about it a number of times, but never seriously" (*The Voice of Memory: Interviews, 1961–1987*, ed. Marco Belpoliti and Robert Gordon, trans. Robert Gordon [New York: New Press, 2001], p. 246). The suicide rate in the camps has been a subject of dispute. Nazi records are unreliable since suicide in the camps was viewed as a form of escape from the captors' control; so, for example, those in the camps who (intentionally or not) walked into prohibited zones which brought death by shooting or into the electrified fences (with the same effect) would be registered as killed while "attempting to escape." Levi recalls that under Fascism in Italy, a party directive banned news of suicides, presumably to sustain popular morale; thus, for example, journalists reporting a suicide by shooting could report only that "the unfortunate citizen who, running through the house or along the street with a loaded pistol . . . fell and was struck by an accidental bullet" (*La Stampa*, May 3, 1986, in Levi, *The Black Hole of Auschwitz*, p. 176). Statistics on suicide in these contexts thus necessarily remain indeterminate. See David Lester, "The Suicide Rate in the Concentration Camps Was Extraordinarily High," *Archives of Suicide Research* 8 (2004): 199–201 and in *American Journal of Psychiatry* (2005): 701–4; see also Jared Stark, "Suicide After Auschwitz," *Yale Journal of Criticism* 14 (2001): 93–114. More is known about the increased rate of suicide *prior* to deportation; see Christian Goetschel, *Suicide in Nazi Germany* (New York: Oxford University Press, 2009).

9. There is also a reference, a telling but (perhaps?) chance allusion, in the last chapter of *If This Is a Man*, where Levi, describing how, after the Germans had abandoned Auschwitz, he and his ten roommates—several suffering from diphtheria (Levi himself had scarlet fever)—who were left in the camp infirmary as unfit for the evacuation march, resisted the efforts of others in the infirmary to enter their heated room despite diphtheria's infectiousness and the fact, in Levi's words, that "to fall ill of diphtheria in these conditions was more surely fatal than jumping off a fourth floor" (the Italian refers to a "third" floor—again, the American fourth).

10. Against this background of possibilities, it is worth noting that in the period of 1887–1993, the rate of suicide in Italy was highest among the age group of sixty-five and over—and the highest rate of suicide during that period occurred during the years 1980–93. Also that among the means used for suicide in the period overall, "jumping" was second to strangulation/hanging—also that among the eight means of suicide measured, jumping had the largest increase in the period 1980–90. See D. De Leo, D. Conforti, and G. Carollo, "A Century of Suicide in Italy: A Comparison Between the Old and the Young," *Suicide and Life-Threatening Behavior* 27, no. 3 (1997): 239–49. A corollary to this would be studies of suicide among Holocaust survivors. The far from complete accounts that have been attempted indicate that the rate of survivor suicide rises after the age of sixty-five. By itself, this accords with a rise in the suicide rate by age *more generally*, but in one study the rate of attempted suicide or "suicide ideation" among Holocaust survivors sixty-five or older has been three times as great as in a control group whose members were over sixty-five but had not been caught up in the Holocaust. (The entire sample used in this study was drawn from the Jewish populace in Israel.) See Yoram Barak, "The Aging of Holocaust Survivors: Myth and Reality—Concerning Suicide," *Israel Medical Association Journal* 9 (March 2007): 196–98.

11. Letter to Hety Schmitt-Maas, cited in Thomson, *Primo Levi*, p. 396.

Chapter 2. The War

Epigraph: "The Pharaoh with the Swastika," *La Stampa*, September 9, 1983, in Levi, *Black Hole of Auschwitz*, p. 76.

1. This definition, which appeared in the third of the laws of the anti-Jewish legislation (no. 1728), was a broadening of the initial two laws (nos. 1390 and 1381) which set as a requirement that *both* parents had to be Jewish.

2. Quoted in Ian Thomson, *Primo Levi: A Life* (New York: Picador, 2002), p. 87.

3. There is some evidence that Leonardo de Benedetti, a physician whom Levi met in Fossoli and with whom he began a

lifelong friendship then, knew even at that early time what Auschwitz was. If he did, however, it would have been unlikely for him not to speak of it to Levi—and Levi implies in *If This Is a Man* that this did not happen.

4. Jan Karski reported the conversation in Claude Lanzmann's film *The Karski Report* (2010).

5. Susan Zuccotti, *Under His Very Windows: The Vatican and the Holocaust in Italy* (New Haven: Yale University Press, 2000).

6. Levi, interview with Paola Valabrega (1981), in *The Voice of Memory: Interviews, 1961–1987*, ed. Marco Belpoliti and Robert Gordon, trans. Robert Gordon (New York: New Press, 2001), p. 27 ("of no account"); Levi, interview with Anna Bravo and Frederico Cereja (1983), ibid., p. 223 ("My experience as a partisan"). Levi's claim here that he was not armed conflicts with his statement elsewhere about the small pistol. The more basic claim that his group as a whole was poorly equipped for combat was unquestionably accurate. Cited in Levi, *Works*, p. lxxviii, where he speaks of the period as the "most opaque of my career."

7. Levi, interview with Paola Valabrega.

8. Levi, "Gold," in *The Periodic Table*, p. 132.

9. So, in "Epitaph" (October 1952): "Here where, dry-eyed, my comrades buried me. . . . / Killed by my companions for no small crimes, / I, Micca the partisan, haven't lain here many years." And still more indeterminate is this in "Partisan" (July 23, 1983): "Like them, we will stand guard / So the enemy will not take us by surprise at dawn, / What enemy? Every man is the enemy of every other, / With everyone split by an inner border, / The right hand enemy of the left." Levi preserves a fuller silence still about another episode of violence to which he almost certainly *was* witness, in his railroad car on the way from Fossoli to Auschwitz. Arturo Foa, a Jewish writer who remained outspoken in his Fascist allegiance even after being interned at Fossoli, entered the car alive and was dead by the journey's end. Levi never wrote about this, but when once asked directly about it, he broke down crying, though still without responding.

10. Ferdinando Camon, *Conversations with Primo Levi*, trans.

John Shepley (Marlboro, Vt.: Marlboro Press, 1989), p. 8. See also Levi's story "Gold" in *The Periodic Table*. In *If This Is a Man*, Levi writes in more practical terms: "I preferred to admit my status as an 'Italian citizen of Jewish race.' I felt that otherwise I would be unable to justify my presence in places too secluded even for an evacuee; while I believed (wrongly as was subsequently seen) that the admission of my political activity would have meant torture and certain death" (pp. 13–14).

11. Levi, *If This Is a Man*, p. 16.

12. Ibid., p. 19.

13. The practice of tattooing numbers on Häftlinge was unique to Auschwitz, not followed in other death or concentration camps. Deportees at Auschwitz who were picked out at the first selection upon their arrival and sent to their deaths immediately were not tattooed or registered. However related to this practice, members of the S.S. were also tattooed in their armpits with the letters of their blood type.

14. Levi, *If This Is a Man*, p. 29.

15. Ibid., pp. 107–8.

16. Ibid., p. 100.

17. See on these issues, e.g., Joshua D. Zimmerman, ed., *Jews in Italy Under Fascist and Nazi Rule, 1922–1945* (Cambridge: Cambridge University Press, 2005); Ruth Ben-Ghiat, "Fascism, Writing, and Memory: The Realist Aesthetic in Italy, 1930–1950," *Journal of Modern History* 67, no. 3 (1995): 627–65; I am also indebted to Ariella Lang's unpublished essay "Troubled Nationalism in Modern Italian-Jewish History."

Chapter 3. Writing

1. Levi, interview with Philip Roth (1986), in *The Voice of Memory: Interviews, 1961–1987*, ed. Marco Belpoliti and Robert Gordon, trans. Robert Gordon (New York: New Press, 2001), p. 18.

2. Levi, interview with Ruita Caccamo De Luca and Manuela Olagnero, 1984, reprinted in *The Black Hole of Auschwitz*, p. 163; Levi, Introduction to R. Höss, *Commandante ad Auschwitz* (Turin: Einaudi, 1985), reprinted in *The Black Hole of Auschwitz*, p. 102.

NOTES TO PAGES 62–85

3. Levi, *Moments of Reprieve*, p. 11; Levi, interview with Graziella Grana (1981), in *The Voice of Memory*. p. 148.

4. "Guido" is described in Ian Thomson, *Primo Levi: A Life* (New York: Picador, 2002), p. 60.

5. Levi, *The Search for Roots*, p. 3.

6. Ibid., p. 5.

7. Ibid., p. 6.

8. Quoted in Peter Forbes, Introduction, ibid., xv ("deliberately excluded names"); Levi, interview with Aurelio Andreoli (1981), in *The Voice of Memory*, p. 102 ("Life is too short"); Levi, interview with Federico De Melis (1983), ibid., pp. 155 ("one of my favorite authors"), 159 ("fears punishment"); Levi, *The Search for Roots*, p. 198 ("no one has the key"); Levi, *Other People's Trades*, p. 173 ("least decipherable poets"); Levi, interview with Ian Thomson (1986), in *The Voice of Memory*, p. 42 ("writing should be a public service"); Levi, interview with Aurelio Andreoli, p. 100 ("alien and distant").

9. Levi, *Other People's Trades*, p. 175 ("clear and useless"); Levi, interview with Aurelio Andreoli, p. 101 ("seems too thin"); Levi, interview with Anthony Rudolf (1986), in *The Voice of Memory*, p. 27 ("Wiesel chose a different path").

10. Levi, *Collected Poems*, pp. 42, 21, 48, 24.

11. Levi, interview with Federico De Melis, p. 156.

12. Levi, *The Monkey's Wrench*, pp. 54, 53, 48.

13. Levi, *Other People's Trades*, p. 221.

14. Ibid., p. 222.

15. In his 1986 interview with Levi, Philip Roth gently summarizes this liability of *If Not Now, When?*: "Your other books are perhaps less imaginary, as to subject matter, but more imaginative in technique. The motive [here] seems more narrowly tendentious—and consequently less liberating" (*The Voice of Memory*, p. 20).

16. Levi, *Other People's Trades*, p. 128.

17. Ibid., p. 15.

18. In an oddly articulated competition that seems itself to have had no previous or subsequent competition, the Royal Institution of Great Britain in 2006 awarded a prize for "The Best Sci-

ence Book Ever Written" to *The Periodic Table*—over the short-list rivals Konrad Lorenz's *King Solomon's Ring*, Tom Stoppard's *Arcadia*, and Richard Dawkins's *The Selfish Gene*. (Darwin's *Voyage of the "Beagle"* had been nominated for the award, but did not make the short list.)

19. Some attempts in this direction have been made. So, for example, in the introduction to the 1997 Einaudi edition of Levi's collected works, Daniele Del Giudice cites in a concluding section Claude Lévi-Strauss's characterization of Levi as a "great ethnographer"—but the plausible grounds for that characterization seem lost even in the great variety of traditional literary categories.

Chapter 4. The Jewish Question

1. Levi, *The Search for Roots*, p. 147.

2. Levi, interview with Germaine Greer (1985), in *The Voice of Memory: Interviews, 1961–1987*, ed. Marco Belpoliti and Robert Gordon, trans. Robert Gordon (New York: New Press, 2001), p. 8.

3. An exemplary moment in this discussion occurred in 2002 when the panel of judges for the Koret Jewish Book awards debated W. G. Sebald's *Austerlitz* as a candidate for the award in literature. The resolution reached at the time was to give Sebald a special award for his contributions to literature; the prize in the "standard" category of fiction among Jewish books published was given to Isaac Babel's *Collected Stories* (stories written and many of them published sixty-five years or more earlier).

4. Levi, "Gold," in *The Periodic Table*, p. 129.

5. Levi, interview with Edith Bruck (1976), in *The Voice of Memory*, p. 263. The Italian term *propaganda* had historical and continuing connotations (including in this reference by Levi) that were less pejorative than its common current English usage. In its early—perhaps earliest—usage (1622) for the ecclesiastical "Congregatio de propaganda fide," for example, and in other subsequent uses, the term refers to propagating or disseminating whatever the action intended is meant to; Levi's reference here should be understood in this context.

6. Levi, interview with Gad Lerner (1984), in *The Voice of Memory*, p. 288.

7. Ferdinando Camon, *Conversations with Primo Levi*, trans. John Shepley (Marlboro, Vt.: Marlboro Press, 1989), p. 55.

8. Levi, Preface, *Gardens and Ghettos: The Art of Jewish Life in Italy*, ed. Vivian Mann (Berkeley: University of California Press, 1989), p. xvii.

Chapter 5. Thinking

1. Levi, *The Search for Roots*, p. 77.

2. Levi, *If This Is a Man*, p. 97.

3. Ibid., p. 87.

4. Ibid., pp. 107–8.

5. Levi, interview with Ian Thomson (1986), in *The Voice of Memory: Interviews, 1961–1987*, ed. Marco Belpoliti and Robert Gordon, trans. Robert Gordon (New York: New Press, 2001), p. 39.

6. Levi, *The Drowned and the Saved*, p. 48.

7. Levi, *If This Is a Man*, pp. 129–30.

8. Ibid., pp. 157–58.

9. Levi, *Other People's Trades*, pp. 212–13.

Chapter 6. The Beginning

1. Levi, interview with Pier Maria Paoletti (1963), in *The Voice of Memory: Interviews, 1961–1987*, ed. Marco Belpoliti and Robert Gordon, trans. Robert Gordon (New York: New Press, 2001), p. 81.

INDEX

Unless otherwise identified, all titles are by Primo Levi.

Maestro, Vanda, 27, 29, 31
Maimonides, Moses, 143
Mann, Thomas, 64
Manzoni, Alessandro, 66
Mayakovsky, Vladimir, 14
Melville, Herman, 65, 66
Mendel, David, 9–10
Momigliano, Paolo, 24
Montaigne, Michel de, 87, 90
Moravia, Alberto, 5
Morpurgo, Beatrice (PL's mother-
	in-law), 2
Muselmann, 8, 133
Mussolini, Benito, 17, 21, 103
	as head of Salo government, 22
	march on Rome by, 19

Neri, Agostino, 7
Nietzsche, Friedrich, 114–15
Nissim, Luciana, 27, 29
Nuremberg Laws, 17–18

Ortona, Silvio, 9
Orwell, George, 74, 87

Paoletti, Pier Maria, 146–47
Pascal, Blaise, 87
Pavese, Cesare, 7, 14
Periodic Table, 84–86, 94–95,
	167–68n18
Perrone, Lorenzo, 7, 33, 41, 120
Perugia, Lello, 66
Piacenza, Aldo, 27
Piedmont, 17, 85, 95
Plath, Sylvia, 14
Plato, 124
Polo, Marco, 65
Pound, Ezra, 67
Presser, Jacques, 74
Proust, Marcel, 68

Rabelais, François, 13, 64, 65,
	152
Roosevelt, Franklin Delano, 22
Rosselli, Carlo, 106
Rosselli, Nello, 106
Roth, Philip, 49, 69, 100, 167n15

Rumkowski, Chaim, 129
Russell, Bertrand, 65

Saba, Umberto, 69
Sacerdote, Enrico (PL's uncle), 7
Sachs, Nelly, 11
Saint-Exupéry, Antoine de, 65
Salmoni, Alberto, 9
Sartre, Jean-Paul, 94
Scholem, Gershom, 99
Search for Roots, 64–69, 96
Sebald, W. G., 168n3
Serenyi, Gitta 122
Serra, Bianca Giudetti, 9
Sharon, Ariel, 108
Sholem Aleichem [Rabinovitch], 64, 96
SIVA (Società industriale vernici e
	affini), 11, 39, 49–51
Snow, C. P., 36, 149–50
Sobibor (camp), 18
Spinoza, Baruch, 124
Stalingrad, Battle of, 17
Stangl, Franz, 122
Stern, Mario Rigoni, 65
Stevens, Wallace, 72
Strunk, William, 71
Survival at Auschwitz. See *If This Is a
	Man*
Svevo, Italo, 50
Swift, Jonathan, 65

Thoreau, Henry David, 87, 90
Trakl, Georg, 67
Treblinka (camp), 18
Truce, 40–42, 151
Turin 18, 43–45, 92, 100, 109–10

Vatican, 19, 23, 43
Vercel, Roger, 65
Voltaire, 137

White, E. B., 71
Wiesel, Elie, 4, 68–69, 86–87, 134
Wilkomirski, Benjamin, 86
Wrench, 76–77, 79

Yeats, William Butler, 72

PHOTOGRAPH CREDITS

Frontispiece: *Gente*, September 20, 1963; Chapter 1, Residents of Corso Re Umberto 75, © 2013 Ari Frankel, www.toscratchan angel.com, all rights reserved; Chapter 2, I. G. Farben complex at Monowitz-Buna (Auschwitz-III), including Buna laboratory: Auschwitz-Birkenau State Museum Archives; Chapter 3, Levi at the typewriter: © Gianni Giansanti/Sygma/Corbis; Chapter 4, Levi with students: © *La Stampa*, property and courtesy of the Levi family; Chapter 5, Levi in Thought: © Jillian Edelstein: Chapter 6, Gravestone of Primo Levi: © 2013 Ari Frankel, www.toscratch anangel.com, all rights reserved.